MOTORCYCLING
For Beginners

MOTORCYCLING
For Beginners

A Manual for Safe Riding

I. G. EDMONDS

MACRAE SMITH COMPANY
Philadelphia

CONTENTS

To Annette

INTRODUCTION

There was a time in the current slang of the day when a young man who was really getting around was called a "wheeler-dealer." Today if we change this old expression to "two-wheeler dealer" we'll be describing a good-sized bite of the present generation.

The "in" thing today is the two-wheel vehicle—the motorcycle. The motorcycle has been around, of course, for a long time. But for half a century it was primarily a utility vehicle and a sport racer for a few hardy souls. Today all that has changed. Since 1950 there has been a tremendous surge of interest in cycling as a growing segment of the country discovered that motorcycling is a "fun" sport and that the two-wheeler is a "fun machine."

We can get an idea of the impact of these fun machines by taking a look at registration figures. In 1930 there were just over 132,000 registered motorcycles in the United States. Twenty-five years later—in 1955—the number had increased some threefold to 415,000. Now rush ahead another seventeen years. Today, according to the

American Motorcycle Association, there are two million registered motorcycles zipping around the United States. These are registered bikes and do not include the many motorcycles, minibikes, trail bikes, and others that are not to be run on the highways and thus do not require registration.

The great boom in cycles began when Honda, the Japanese motorcycle manufacturer, began an aggressive campaign to popularize cycling in the mid-1950's. However, motorcycles have been around so long that they can look at Detroit's four-wheel chariots and call them "Johnnie-come-latelies." The motorcycle's mom and pop were bicycles, and bicycles go back to 1690.

The entire history of the human race is the story of man's search for ways to avoid walking. The first transportation invention was probably a floating log used by the caveman to paddle himself across a stream. Later he found that if the log was hollowed into a dugout canoe he would have better control and swifter motion in water. Next was the domestication and training of animals he could ride and thus move faster and farther on land.

Then came the invention of the wheel, the basic invention of all subsequent mechanisms. All science, invention, and civilization are rooted in this truly revolutionary development. In time the wheel, which probably began as a roller log used to make heavy burdens slip more easily, grew into the chariot, ox cart, wagon, and buggy.

Then in 1690 the never-ending search to find mechanical means to avoid walking produced the *celerifère*. It was thought up by an inventor in France. It was simply a wooden beam with a wheel attached to each end. The rider sat on a cushion midway between the wheels. He propelled himself by pushing his feet against the ground. There was no means of steering except by dragging one's feet. It became a popular sport to coast downhill on the things.

These "walking machines" continued without improvement until 1816 when Germany's Karl von Drais invented his *Draisienne.* This was only the familiar walking machine with handlebars and a pivoting front wheel. The rider still propelled the machine by pushing his feet on the ground. The Draisienne was imported to England where it became known as the Hobby Horse.

Thirteen years later a Frenchman put pedals on the front wheel of the Draisienne, but this was not successful since there was no gearing and the rider could not get any speed, as the pedal had to make one revolution for each revolution of the wheel. Then in 1855 another Frenchman reduced the amount of pedaling by enlarging the front wheel and reducing the back wheel.

This sparked new interest. The machine that began as the *celerifère,* then became the Draisienne, the Hobby

An ancestor of the motorcycle was the Draisienne, invented by Baron Karl von Drais in 1816, shown in this nineteenth-century lithograph.

Horse, and finally the bicycle, got a new name: the "boneshaker." The wooden wheels were shod with iron and the jolting on the cobblestone paving of day restricted its use to the hardiest of souls.

Things got better in 1869 when an Englishman replaced the iron tires with solid rubber ones. This same year two French brothers, Pierre and Ernest Michaux, pointed the way to the future motorcycle when they put a steam engine on the walking machine.

Shortly after this, Englishman James Starley produced the first really popular walking machine. He enlarged the front wheel three times and reduced the rear one to about 18 inches in diameter. The pedals were attached directly to the large front wheel without sprocket or chain. The extraordinarily large front wheel permitted fast speeds—if one could stay upright—and bicycle racing became a rage in Europe.

Finally in 1880 the sprocket-and-chain drive was invented, which permitted reducing the dangerously large front wheel to the same size as the back wheel. The new bicycle was known as the "safety cycle." It brought bicycling to the peak of interest. By 1899 the United States alone was producing a million cycles a year.

Although attempts had been made to put steam engines on bicycles, none had been really successful. The invention of the motorcycle had to wait for the development of a reliable internal combustion engine. Credit for finally solving the problem goes to Gottlieb Daimler of Germany. Daimler, who gave his name to a famous automobile, put a one-cylinder benzine-fueled engine on a specially made bicycle. The engine was connected to the rear wheel. Fuel had to be heated in a glass tube to

This 1912 Indian racing machine, built for the factory's racing team, shows how the motorcycle has grown over the years. Note the complete lack of suspension. The rider had a hard ride.

This 1921 Moto-Guzzi, Italian-built racer, won the first race it entered. Compared with the 1912 Indian, one can see the enormous strides made in motorcycle building in just nine years.

provide the initial fire. It was started by the driver's pushing the cycle to turn over the cylinders. Once the machine was started, the driver leaped astraddle and took off. This grandfather of all motorcycles is still preserved in the Mercedes-Benz museum in Germany.

In time the motorcycle developed improved engines, better suspension and carburetion patterned after the automobile. Public acceptance came slowly. Industrial companies found them money-savers. They became popular as delivery cars; the Bell Telephone Company bought 700 to use in checking lines. At the same time the U.S. Army found them extremely valuable for carrying dispatches. They became highly useful to city police forces as automobile traffic increased.

The big spurt in general public acceptance came after World War I. Many soldiers either drove cycles as couriers or came into contact with them while in the service. They brought back their interest to civilian life just as soldiers of World War II made the Jeep a commercial success after the war.

Interest continued to grow slowly, but it was Honda's aggressive drive to prove that motorcycling was fun that started the sport booming in the United States and convinced a lot of doubters that cycling was not the dangerous sport that many thought it to be.

For a few years wild gangs riding motorcycles gave the sport a black eye, but strict law enforcement and public pressure have greatly restricted such lawless groups. Today the "Wild Bunch" and the "Easy Rider" class are strictly in the minority. Most motorcycle clubs are composed of serious young people who have banded together for the sole purpose of staging fun events, such as hill climbs, Hare and Hounds races, Moto-Cross, time trials, and even drag racing.

A major reason for the growing enthusiasm for cycling is that, as in horseback riding and polo, the man and his mount form a coordinated team. As enthusiastic riders put it, you and the machine grow together.

Other things, of course, have contributed to motorcycling's present popularity. One is the relatively inexpensive cost of good machines and low cost of operation. While gas mileage varies, one-cylinder machines may get up to 60 miles per gallon while the new four-cylinder road bikes don't do much better than the average subcompact automobile.

Another reason for the growing popularity of motorcycles is the sense of freedom one gets riding them. The growth of organized motorcycle sports has also helped the bike boom.

A drawback has been the public belief that motorcycling is particularly dangerous. Generally speaking, the accident rate for motorcycles is about four times that of cars. Recently in its pre-Labor Day publicity the Federal National Transportation Safety Board claimed that the number of death attributable to motorcycle accidents had jumped from 1,960 in 1969 to 2,330 in 1970.

John H. Reed, the Safety Board's chairman, said that roughly two-thirds of these cycling casualties have been in the 15–24 year age group. This is also the most dangerous age group for automobile drivers.

Motorcyclists themselves deny that their sport is as dangerous as the public, reading statistics like those of the Safety Board, believes. They claim that motorcycling is no more dangerous than driving a car *if the rider knows what he is doing and takes proper safety precautions.*

   Far too many new riders are joining the ranks of the nation's motorcyclists without proper safety instruction. In the hands of such inexperienced riders motorcycles are definitely dangerous. And this danger begins even before you start the machine moving. You can break a leg just kicking the starter improperly.
   The secret of safe motorcycling can be summed up in these general rules:

- *KNOW WHAT YOU'RE DOING.* This means understanding your bike and its limitations and getting proper instruction before making your first ride.

- *KEEP CONSTANTLY ALERT WHILE RIDING.* This means watching out for natural road hazards, including car drivers. More than a quarter of accidents involving motorcycles are the fault of car drivers. A motorcycle seat is no place for a day dreamer.

- *KEEP YOUR BIKE IN GOOD CONDITION.* Next to inattention while riding, poor mechanical condition of bikes is responsible for more spills than any other single factor.

- *LEAVE STUNTING TO PROFESSIONAL STUNT MEN.*

- *LEARN AND FOLLOW THE SAFETY RULES OF THE ROAD.*

In motorcycling only the safe rider is a good rider. And the purpose of this book is to teach some of the rules for becoming a good and safe rider. Safety on two wheels does not mean proceeding down the road like the car salesman's proverbial Little Old Lady from Pasadena. The road turtle is as dangerous as the road hog or the highway jackrabbit. Safety does not mean sacrificing any of the fun and freedom that has been responsible for so many young people's taking to the two-wheel fun machines.

At races you will see a driver "lay over" his machine until it almost appears that he is horizontal. At a Moto-Cross you'll see cycles bouncing like two-wheeled pogo sticks. On Cross-Countries they zip through roadless back country as if they were on a paved highway. Startling as some of these action appear to watch, they are not dangerous because the driver is experienced and knows exactly what he is doing.

So safe riding does not mean that one must give up drag racing, hill climbs, rallies, Moto-Crosses, time trials, or any fun activities that have made motorcycling one of the fastest-growing sports in America today.

Part 1:

CYCLE SAFETY

Chapter 1

WHAT MAKES IT RUN?

"How do I turn on the ignition?"

This is the question most beginners ask as they approach a bike for the first ride. It is a necessary question, of course, but it should be about the ten-thousandth question a beginner asks and not the first one.

It is a mistake to assume that because one can ride a bicycle one can automatically ride a motorcycle. Taking off without proper instruction is one of the reasons a beginner finds himself picking up the pieces of his new bike—or worse, finding someone picking *him* up.

The First Question

The first questions a beginner should ask is, "What makes it run?" No one should try to ride a cycle until he understands thoroughly the principles of the motorcycle engine, transmission, clutch, brakes, and controls. More than one inexperienced rider has climbed on an unfamiliar cycle and a second later found himself lying on the asphalt. Even an experienced rider has to familiarize himself with a new machine. While controls are becoming

3

standardized on most machines, there are still some around that have things reversed.

To call a motorcycle a bicycle with an engine is to simplify things too much. It is better to call a cycle an automobile that has been reduced to two wheels. Convertible, of course. On today's motorcycles you can get multicylinders, four-stroke (cycle) engines, tachometers, electric starters, flashing turn signals, disc brakes, and many other refinements developed first for the four-wheel chariots.

A recent list of manufacturers showed more than forty companies that make lightweight cycles and over thirty that build road and touring models. With this many builders there is naturally a great deal of variation between models. However, they all use the same basic principles. If you understand how one motorcycle works in general, you will know how all of them work, even though individual machines have peculiarities of their own which must also be learned.

While there are many kinds of motorcycles, each type is designed for a specific purpose. No one cycle can satisfactorily do all kinds of work. A big-bore road hog is not satisfactory for trail riding. It is too big. Nor does a trail bike have the power for road racing. And so on.

Although the beginner is faced with a bewildering selection of motorcycles, basically they can be divided into two classifications: two-stroke and four-stroke engines. (Two-cycle and four-cycle are other names for the same thing.) These terms describe the principle of the engine used and have nothing to do with the size, efficiency, or power of the engines.

The two-cycle engine is the simpliest of all internal

combustion engines. They are found on lawnmowers, outboard motorboats, and lightweight motorcycles. By lightweight bikes we mean those up to 250 cubic centimeters (cc) displacement. The four-stroke engine is used on larger motorcycles and automobiles.

Since most beginners start on the smaller displacement machines, he will most likely come in contact with the two-cycle engine first. However, since the four-stroke engine is so widely used and many beginners have some

Careful riding does not mean crawling down the road. Here the cyclist in the foreground is literally flying his bike as he struggles to get ahead of his competitor in a Moto-Cross run. Yet he is driving safely because he understands his machine and is dressed to take the shock if he does slip.

Norton Hi-Rider
750 cc

Motorcycle Nomenclature

A   front wheel brake control lever
B   gas throttle built into right hand grip
    *(Left and right here is from the riders'
    position not the viewer's.)*
C   spark control in left hand grip
D   clutch control lever
E   speedometer
F   tachometer
G   gas tank
H   saddle or seat
I, J   front fork
K   carburetor
L   engine
M   engine air cleaner

N   rear suspension spring
O   oil tank
P   front fender
Q   exhaust pipe
R   rear-wheel brake
S   foot peg
T   muffler
U   front-wheel brake drum

familiarity with it through association with automobiles, we will consider it first.

Internal combustion engines, both two-cycle and four-cycle, have this much in common: they are built around a *block* of metal in which is bored a round hole known as a *cylinder*. An engine may have as few as one cylinder or as many as twelve working as a team.

The open top of the cylinder is closed with a *cylinder head*. The bottom of the cylinder is closed with a *piston*.

This piston is joined to a crankshaft by means of a *connecting rod.* The rod is fitted around an off-center journal on the crankshaft so that the piston is raised and lowered in the cylinder as the crankshaft revolves. Rings fitted around the piston provide a gas-tight seal between the piston and the cylinder walls.

Now when the piston is drawn to its lowest position in the cylinder by the revolving crankshaft, a mixture of air and gas is fed into the cylinder. As the crankshaft turns, the piston rises in the cylinder. This compresses the air-gas mixture into a small space where a spark from a spark plug set in the cylinder head ignites the fuel mixture. The burning gases expand with sudden and terrific force. This force pushes the piston down and the power is transferred through the connecting rod to force the crankshaft to spin. The rotation of the crankshaft raises the piston again and the firing cycle is repeated as long as the engine is running.

The power or *torque* (which is a turning force) created in the crankshaft is transmitted through the clutch, gears, and transmission to the rear wheels of the vehicle to make it move.

This, in very simplest terms, is how an internal combustion engine works. However, the operation is is not as simple as it sounds. There are a number of supporting actions which must work just right before an engine can develop sufficient power to run either a motorcycle or an automobile. They are such problems as how to get gas into the cylinder, how much air should be mixed with the gas to make it burn, how much to compress the mixture to get full power, at what point the ignition should fire the fuel, and how to get the burned gases out of the cylinder so a fresh charge of fuel can be admitted.

Some of these problems are solved by making the crankshaft revolve several times for each firing. These extra revolutions are what give the four-stroke engine its name. These engines do not fire each time the piston moves. The piston must make four moves—two up and two down for each firing of the fuel.

A Frenchman named Alphonse Beau de Rochas invented the four-stroke engine in 1862, but it was not too successful. Later it was improved by a German named Nikolaus Otto, giving us the basic engine that is still used today.

This Honda 350 is a typical example of a modern four-stroke motorcycle engine. Major parts include carburetor (A), fuel line (B), cutoff valve (C), throttle cable (D), air cleaner (E), clutch cable (F), spark plug (G), exhaust pipe (H), sprocket gear (I), and drive chain (J).

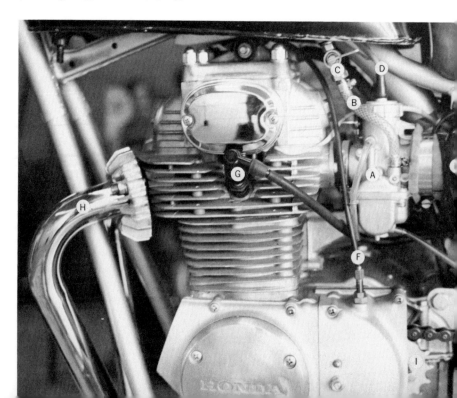

The four-stroke engine works like this:

First stroke. The piston is pulled down in the cylinder by the turning of the crankshaft. Before the engine fires, this turning of the crankshaft is done in a motorcycle either with the *kick starter* (a kind of foot-operated crank) or by an electric starter motor. This stroke is completed when the piston descends as far as possible into the cylinder. This point is known as *bottom dead center* or, in the lingo of automotive people, BDC. The revolving crankshaft operates a cam, which pushes upward on a pushrod to open the engine's *intake valve.* The descending piston causes a lowered air pressure or partial vacuum in the cylinder. This causes the air-gas mixture that comprises the fuel to be sucked into the cylinder. At BDC the valve closes, trapping the air-gas mixture in the cylinder. This is the *intake stroke.*

Second stroke. When the piston reaches BDC the first stroke of the four-stroke cycle is completed. The revolving crankshaft now raises the piston in the cylinder again. The air-gas fuel mixture trapped in the cylinder is squeezed or compressed into a small area in the cylinder head known as the *combustion chamber.* This stroke is complete when the piston reaches *top dead center* or TDC. This is the *compression stroke.* It is very important, since loosely packed fuel has little power when it burns. The more the fuel is compressed the greater will be its force when it burns. This is why high-performance engines are always high-compression engines.

Third stroke. This is the power stroke and is the payoff. Slightly before the piston reaches TDC, a spark from the spark plug ignites the fuel mixture. The resulting expansion of burning gases then reach a properly timed peak to start exerting pressure on the piston when the piston reaches TDC. If the ignition is too early—a condition known as preignition—the expanding gases try to push the piston down at the same time that the crankshaft is trying to push it up. If preignition is severe, it can destroy the engine.

The expanding gases push the piston to BDC, completing the power stroke. The force of the piston descending keeps the crankshaft spinning.

Fourth stroke. The final stroke in the four-stroke cycle is the *exhaust stroke.* The piston starts to rise immediately after reaching BDC on the previous power stroke. At the same time the camshaft causes the exhaust valve to open. As the piston rises on this stroke the burned gases are pushed out of the cylinder and into the exhaust. The piston continues to TDC, the exhaust valve closes, and the four-stroke cycle is complete. The cycle is repeated as long as the engine is running.

Vaporizing the Gasoline

This description has been based upon the description of a one-cylinder engine. If the cycle has two cylinders, they are both connected to the crankshaft and work as a team. The method of introducing fuel into the cylinders may be done by either of two methods. One is the Otto cycle and the other is the Diesel cycle. In the Otto cycle a carburetor is used to vaporize the gasoline before it goes into the cylinder. Liquid gasoline will not burn in the engine but must be mixed with the proper amount of air before it will ignite.

The carburetor vaporizes or atomizes the gasoline by using the venturi principle. A venturi is simply a pipe that

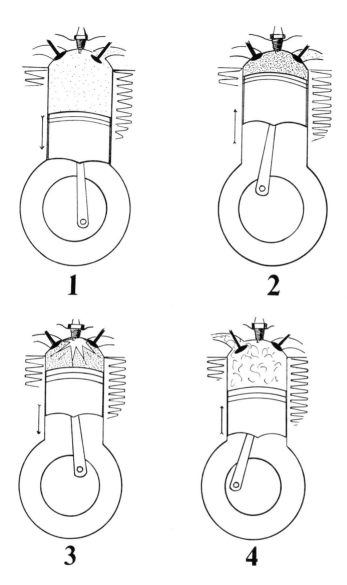

Principle of the four-stroke engine. *On* stroke one *the piston is pulled down by the turning crankshaft. At the same time the intake valve opens and the fuel-air mix from the carburetor is drawn into the cylinder.* Stroke two *is when the piston goes up again. With both intake and exhaust valves closed, the fuel-air mix is compressed into the small area of the combustion chamber at the top of the cylinder.* Stroke three *is the power stroke. The burning gas, ignited by the spark plug, forces the piston down, transferring power to the crankshaft.* Stroke four *is the exhaust stroke. The rising piston pushes the burned gases out through the open exhaust valve.*

has its center section squeezed down smaller than its two ends. It is a principles of physics that air flowing through such a tube will *increase* in speed as it flows through the restricted part of the tube, but will *decrease* in pressure. This low pressure creates a vacuum condition. Fuel from the reservoir or bowl of the carburetor, which is at normal air pressure, is sucked into the fast-moving stream of air by the low-pressure vacuum in the venturi. This vaporizes the gasoline, making it suitable for burning in the engine. This vaporized air-gas mixture is then pulled into the cylinders through the intake ports of the engine. Here it is ignited (in the Otto cycle) by a spark from a spark plug which draws its current from either a battery or a magneto.

Cross section of a British BMW 250-cc one-cylinder engine shows major parts of a four-stroke engine:

A rocker arm	*G exhaust port*
B exhaust valve and spring	*H connecting rod*
C exhaust valve pushrod	*I piston*
D intake valve pushrod	*J timing chain and gears*
E intake valve	*K crankshaft*
F carburetor	*L flywheel*
	M camshaft

The Diesel Cycle

The Diesel cycle accomplishes the same thing by an entirely different means. On the intake stroke of the Otto-cycle engine, the air-gas mixture is pulled into the cylinder, but on the Diesel-cycle engine only air is pulled into the cylinder. Then on the second or compression stroke, the air is highly compressed by the rising piston just as the air-gas mix is compressed in the Otto-cycle engine.

Now it is another principle of physics that compression creates heat. The Diesel-cycle engine takes advantage of this heat build-up in the cylinder. Just before the piston reaches TDC, liquid gasoline is injected (squirted) into the cylinder. It mixes with the air being compressed and the mixture is ignited by the heat of the compressed air.

This type of engine does not need the spark plug and ignition system necessary in the Otto-cycle engine.

It should be remembered that although the Diesel-cycle engine uses a different method of injecting fuel into the cylinder and igniting the fuel, it is still a four-stroke engine.

The Two-Stroke Engine

The two-stroke engine operates in the same manner as the four-stroke engine in that it takes an air-gas mixture into the cylinder or cylinders, compresses the mixture, and then ignites it to produce the "push" on the pistons that creates torque in the crankshaft.

The big difference is that this engine completes the operation in two strokes during one revolution of the crankshaft. None of the four necessary steps—intake, compression, power, and exhaust—is omitted. Some of them are combined so that all are accomplished during the two strokes—one up and one down.

This results in a far simplier engine with less moving parts. It eliminates the need for cams, moving valves, and pushrods. In fact, the only moving parts in a two-stroke engine are the piston, connecting rod, and crankshaft.

Operation of the Two-Stroker

The familiar poppet valves of the four-cycle engine are replaced in the simpliest type of two-stroke engine by three ports. The *inlet port* opens into the *crankcase,* bringing the air-gas mix from the carburetor into the area *below* the piston instead of above it as in the four-stroker.

Then a *transfer port* directs the fuel mix from the crankcase to the cylinder. Another port opens later to allow the exhaust to escape from the cylinder after the mix is fired.

There are no valves on these ports. The moving piston acts as a moving valve to cover and uncover them at the proper time.

Reference to the accompanying drawings will make the two-stroke cycle more clear. For the purpose of illustration, let's consider the cycle beginning with the piston at BDC.

As the piston rises in the cylinder it compresses the fuel mixture in the cylinder. At the same time, the rising of the piston creates a low pressure in the crankcase. The rising piston uncovers the inlet port. Vaporized fuel from the carburetor flows through the inlet port into the crankcase.

A few degrees before the piston reaches TDC (the exact number of degrees depends upon the engine timing) a spark across the terminals of the spark plug ignites the compressed fuel mixture in the cylinder. The piston reaches TDC, ending the first stroke.

The piston is forced down by the power of the expanding gases to begin the second and final stroke of the cycle. This movement of the piston downward presses against the fresh fuel vapor in the crankcase, compressing it. At the same time the downward movement of the piston uncovers the exhaust port between the cylinder and the exhaust pipe. The burned gases begin flowing out the exhaust port. The descending piston has blocked the inlet port so that no more fuel flows into the crankcase. As the piston continues to descend it uncovers the transfer port. Compressed fuel mix in the crankcase then flows through the transfer port into the cylinder. The incoming fuel helps push the remainder of the exhaust gases out the exhaust port. The piston reaches BDC to end the stroke, completing the two-stroke cycle.

The spinning crankshaft now starts to raise the piston for a new two-stroke cycle. The fuel which has entered the cylinder through the transfer port during the final stroke of the previous cycle is now compressed by the rising piston, ignited and burned to push the piston down for another power stroke, and so on as long as the engine is running.

The Two-Stroke Oil System

Another major difference between the four-stroke and the two-stroke motorcycle is the method of lubricating the inside of the engine. The four-stroke has an oil-pump system something like that of an automobile. The two-stroke engine is lubricated by mixing oil with the gasoline in the fuel tank.

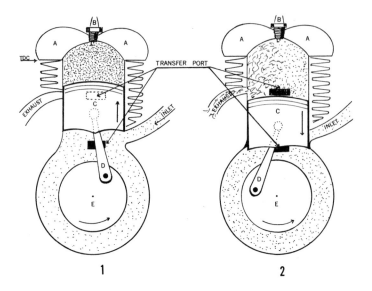

1   2

How a two-stroke engine works. *On stroke one in a two-stroke cycle engine the piston C is raised in the cylinder by the turn of the crankshaft E. The rising piston shuts off the exhaust port and closes the top of the transport port. The open transport ports are shown as black squares and the closed one behind the piston is shown as a dash-line square. At the same time the rising piston uncovers the inlet port and fresh fuel enters into the crankcase while the rising piston greatly compresses the fuel mixture already in the cylinder. Just before the piston reaches TDC, the sparkplug B in the cylinder head A produces a spark which ignites the mixture in the cylinder. The stroke ends when the piston reaches TDC.*

On Stroke two the pressure of the burning gases force the piston down again, transferring power to the crankshaft E. In descending, the piston uncovers the exhaust port and closes the inlet port. As the burned gases start to leave the cylinder, the still descending piston uncovers the transport port. This permits fresh fuel mix to rise from the crankcase where it has been partially compressed by the descending piston pushing against it. The fresh fuel pouring from the top transport port helps scavenge the final remains of the exhaust from the cylinder. The stroke ends when the piston reaches BDC (as far as it can descend into the cylinder). Then a new cycle begins.

The Motesa is a lightweight two-stroke engine. Some of the major parts are:

A gas cutoff valve
B ignition coil
C ignition wire
D spark plug
E cylinder head
F throttle cable
G Air cleaner
H carburetor
I cooling fins on cylinder block
J kick starter

K gearshift lever
L foot peg
M gear box
N body frame

Some beginners are astonished by this oil and gas mixture. They wonder how the machine keeps from burning the oil along with the gas. The answer is simple enough. Most of the oil is separated from the gasoline in the crankcase by the centrifugal force of the flywheels on the crankshaft. You might say it is separated in somewhat the same manner as cream is separated from milk in a separator. As the mixture is spun rapidly, the heavier oil is separated from the lighter gasoline.

The separated oil is hurled against the walls of the crankcase, where it drains into special pockets and is channeled to the bearings. The small amount of oil that does not separate is deposited as a mist on the walls of the cylinder to lubricate it.

Which Is Better?

Each type of engine has its particular advantages. The two-stroke is lighter and therefore favored in lightweight cycles up to 250 cubic centimeters (cc) of displacement. The four-stroke has greater power per cubic centimeter of displacement and is favored for the bigger bikes. Most experts seem to agree that in the below 250-cc classes the two types stand pretty much together and a choice between them is generally a matter of opinion.

There are certain disadvantages to both. The two-stroke, with fewer moving parts, does not have the valve trouble that can develop in the four-stroke engine. But at the same time the two-stroker is more prone to "carbon up," requiring a periodic cleanout. Carbon trouble is more prevalent on street bikes that travel a lot at slow speeds. Fast runs have a tendency to blow out a lot of the carbon.

The carbon comes from the gasoline, which is a hydro-carbon compound. The hydrogen (the "hydro" part of the combination) burns more easily than the carbon, some of which is left as a deposit inside the engine. Excess carbon left in the cylinders retains heat. Glowing particles of this carbon can set off the fuel mixture in the cylinder before the plug fires, causing premature detonation, or preignition.

Since the two-stroke fires twice as fast as the four-stroke engine, it uses more gasoline, and your mileage will not be as good as with the four-stroker. Also the two-stroker is not as efficient an engine, since the exhaust and transfer ports are open at the same time. This results in some of the fuel escaping unburned through the exhaust.

On the other hand, the simpler two-stroke engine is easier to work on, and a beginner who wants to learn to be his own mechanic will find it an advantage in this respect.

Chapter 2

YOUR FIRST "RIDE"

Motorcycle controls are built to pack a lot into small packages. As a result, you'll find your hand and foot doing twice the work they do in driving a car. Motorcycle controls are simple to operate, and once you get used to them they provide a safety margin that you don't have in a car.

The first thing your riding instructor will probably do is ask you to take a "dry run." This means climbing into the saddle and going through the motions of driving. This permits you to learn the controls and develop some proficiency before you start rolling. Motorcycle controls can vary from maker to maker, but in October 1970 the U.S. Government issued a proposed set of standards which will force manufacturers to put their gearshifts, brake pedals, and other important controls in the same place. This won't help change older models, so when we speak here of a brake or pedal being on the left or right side, just remember we are speaking generally. (And "left" or "right" are from the rider's position, not the viewer's.)

When you get on a bike, make sure you familiarize yourself with where everything is.

The Throttle Control

The first thing you must do is learn the position and names of each control. The *throttle* is built into the right handgrip and is operated by twisting your wrist to rotate the control. This rotation operates a cable that regulates the flow of gas in the carburetor. Turning the throttle *toward you* increases speed. Turning the throttle grip *away from you* cuts your speed.

The right hand controls the throttle which is built into the handgrip, and the fingers can reach out quickly and grip the lever that controls the front-wheel brake.

You don't have to know how to drive a car to drive a cycle. Car drivers have an advantage in having some familiarity with a mechanical vehicle and in a knowledge of road safety, but experience has shown that a raw beginner in mechanical transportation sometimes does better than an old-timer. He has not developed automatic reflexes for certain actions. For example, a friend of mine decided after 20 years of driving a car that he would join the legion of trail bike riders. He bought a machine, took proper instructions, and set to conquer the wilds on his mechanical mount. He got along great until he began to lose speed on a steep upgrade. He reacted as he would in an automobile. Without conscious thought, his foot jammed down where years of driving experience told him the gas throttle should be. Only it happened to be the brake on the trail bike. The cycle stopped. He didn't.

A Thinking Man's Machine

This incident points up the fact that a motorcycle is, as I recall an instructor saying years ago, "a thinking man's machine." You can never allow yourself to fall into the reflex rut. Riding a motorcycle means keeping your mind on the job in hand.

After you have learned the position and feel of the throttle, you next learn the position and feel of the front brake lever. It is located along with the throttle on the right handlebar. The fingers of the right hand can grip it easily without removing the hand from the throttle. The brake lever should be adjusted so that your wrist is straight when your hand grips throttle and brake. This gives you better control and is less tiring.

This front brake is supplemented by a foot-operated rear wheel brake. The brake pedal is located just ahead of the foot peg (or rest) so that it can be actuated by a simple downward pressure of the toe of your foot. Unlike driving a car, there is no need to pull your foot off the floor and slam it on the brake in an emergency. A simple shift of your foot downward is sufficient.

When you have learned the position and operation of the two brakes, you move on to the clutch. This essential part of the cycle is a mechanical connection between the motorcycle engine and the final drive. It permits power to be instantly cut off to the main sprocket drive and the rear wheel.

Location of the Clutch

The motorcycle clutch is operated by a hand lever on the left handlebar. It is the twin of the brake lever on the right side of the cycle. Squeezing the lever transmits force through a cable to the clutch inside the transmission housing attached to the engine.

The clutch is an essential element in gear shifting. Gears are provided in the transmission to increase power to the rear wheel. In a direct drive (without a geared

The clutch-control lever is on the opposite or left side and is so located that the palm and thumb can still hold the handlebar grip as the fingers actuate the squeeze on the clutch. The clutch is actuated by a cable that runs from the clutch lever, shown here, to the transmission.

transmission) the back wheel would turn at the same speed as the flywheel on the crankshaft. It so happens that in mechanical engines the greater the speed of rotation the less is the developed power. The direct drive would be fine for high-speed running, but greater power is needed for starting and for tougher grinds such as hill climbing, sand, or mud. For these conditions the ratio of the engine turnover to the spin of the wheel is changed to give greater power to the main sprocket drive. This increased power is obtained at a loss of speed. This is why an automobile runs slower in low gear and faster in second, reaching its greatest speed in high. It is the same with a motorcycle.

The motorcycle clutch also provides a means of control known as "slipping the clutch." This operation, which consists only of partially releasing the clutch under certain conditions, is an automobile "crime" leading to a quickly worn clutch. Motorcycle clutches are more strongly built and can therefore be slipped to help prevent "lugging" or jerkiness at slow speeds. Slipping the clutch is described more fully in Chapter 3.

Shifting Gears

Because it is necessary to have different gears to take care of different speeds and loads, a means of changing from one gear to the other must be provided. This is done on the motorcycle by means of a gearshift lever attached to the gear box. It is foot-operated and is located just in front of the foot peg on the side of the cycle opposite to the brake pedal. Under the new federal motor vehicle safety standards, all gearshifts would be on the left side of the cycle. The location is such that the rider can oper-

The gearshift pedal is on the left side of the Honda just ahead of the riding peg. You go to a lower gear by pressing it down one full stroke and go to a higher gear by slipping your toe under the lever and pulling up one full stroke.

ate the gearshift lever merely by shifting his foot. You shift to a higher gear by slipping your toe under the lever and pulling up. Pressing down on the gearshift lever changes to a lower gear.

Your dry run on gears should be restricted to learning the position of the gearshift and how it works, since you should never actually shift gears unless the motor is running. The shifting parts are not lined up properly unless the transmission is running.

A downward push on the gearshift lever or an upward pull will change only one gear at a time. For example, if you are riding in high gear (and you have a three-speed forward transmission), you down-shift to low by first depressing the lever to move to second, then depressing it again to move to low.

Finding Neutral

Finding neutral, the position where the cycle is out of gear, is very important. On multigear machines beginners often find it difficult to put the cycle out of gear. Neutral position may vary on different machines. Often it is the position between low and second. In this case, low is the last position you can reach by pushing the pedal down. Then to shift from low to neutral, lift the pedal one half-stroke. From second, neutral is a half-stroke down.

It is important to remember that the shift pedal must be allowed to return to its normal central position after each shift before shifting again. The transmission will not shift unless this is done.

Safety Devices

After familiarizing yourself with the parts of a cycle that make it go, you should learn the position of those essentials that are put on for safety. Learn the position of the horn button, how to turn on the lights and dim them for approaching traffic, the operation of your turn signals if the machine is so equipped (if not, learn your hand signals), how the speedometer works, and above all, how the brakes work.

It would appear that learning how to operate the brakes would be self-evident. However, it is a rare motorcycle instructor who does not have a dire tale to tell of beginners who have started their first rides without the foggiest notiton of how to stop. We began this "dry run" talking about brakes, and there is no need to apologize for coming back to them again and again. As one experienced rider said, "Brakes are more important than the engine. You can always *push* your bike, but you can't always stop by dragging your feet!"

The rear wheel brake is operated by a foot pedal on the right side of the cycle. Like the gearshift pedal on the opposite side, it is operated by pressing down with the toe of the shoe without the necessity for removing the foot from the riding peg.

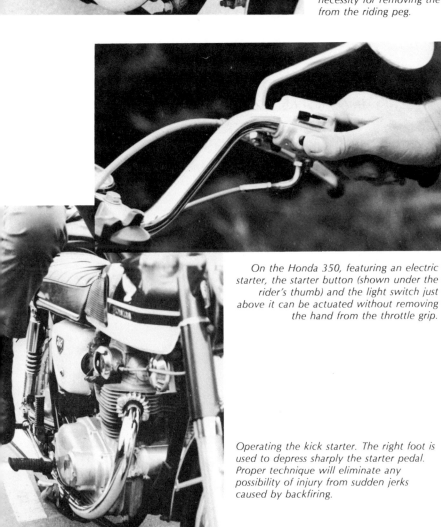

On the Honda 350, featuring an electric starter, the starter button (shown under the rider's thumb) and the light switch just above it can be actuated without removing the hand from the throttle grip.

Operating the kick starter. The right foot is used to depress sharply the starter pedal. Proper technique will eliminate any possibility of injury from sudden jerks caused by backfiring.

The Kick Starter

More and more cycles are now available with electric starters. With these machines it is only necessary to turn on the ignition and press the starter button.

If an engine is cold it will be necessary to use the choke. The choke, which enriches the fuel mixture for easier starting, is generally located on the carburetor and can easily be reached with your hand. Warm engines generally do not require choking.

All engines should be started with the gearshift in neutral and with the clutch engaged.

The most familiar way to start a motorcycle engine is with the kick starter. This is a foot-operated pedal lever on the right side of the engine. It is carried normally folded up out of the way. It operates like the old-fashioned automobile crank, except that the rider uses his foot.

Kicking It Over

Another way in which the kick starter resembles the old-fashioned automobile crank is its ability to kick back. Down through the automobiling years quite a few broken arms have resulted from the kick of a Model T Ford starting crank. The result of a motorcycle backfire (essentially what a kick is) is to knock the starter pedal up violently, which on some bikes can drive your right knee up hard against the handlebar.

The California Highway Patrol, with millions of miles of motorcycling to back up its teaching methods, has this to say about operating a kick starter:

"Injuries from backfiring can be avoided by holding the knee in the locked position, and putting the full weight of your body into the kick."

Follow Through on the Kick

"Backfiring (the report continues) may occur *after* you have completed a through kick, when the starter pedal is at the bottom in the disengaged position. If the engine is spinning backward (as it will on a backfire), and if you start to release the kick starter, the pawl will be violently engaged (knocking your leg upward).

"This can be avoided by holding the kick starter pedal all the way down until the engine either has started or has ceased sound and motion after backfiring."

The Highway Patrol also has another warning about starting:

"Experience has shown that many novices will kick

Instructor Jack Lahn shows the first step in learning to start your cycle. Sit firmly in the saddle, balancing with your two feet while your hands familiarize themselves with the throttle, spark control, front-brake hand lever and clutch-control lever.

their starters in such a way that the inside of their right thigh is rubbed hard against the edge of the saddle. A number of such scrapings will turn the body area black and blue, producing pain, swelling, and subsequent stiffness."

This can be avoided by shifting the weight of your body sufficiently to the right that your leg goes straight down without touching the saddle.

Comfort Means Added Safety

The discomfort caused by repeated hard rubs against the saddle brings up another important safety tip. It would appear that bruising your thigh is a personal discomfort only. But is also classified under the heading of unsafe operation.

For many years both the U.S. Air Force and aircraft manufacturers have maintained what they call "human factors" engineers. One of the most important functions of this work is considering pilot comfort. Experience has shown that if a strap is too tight, a seat uncomfortable, or a control in an awkward place, the pilot can be distracted. At the fast speeds of modern aircraft, a plane can travel a great distance during the short time that the pilot's attention is diverted to his troubles. The same thing is true of a motorcycle. Anything that takes your mind off your driving is bad. Inattention, as we'll learn later when considering road hazards, is an invitation to trouble.

Proper Riding Position

Equally important is how you sit your saddle. The best riding position for road running is a military stance: sit square in the saddle with stomach pulled in, shoulders back and chest out.

This is not regimentation. On long rides this position is less fatiguing than a slump. Also, a slump puts greater strain on a rider's kidneys. When the back is straight your kidneys are supported by the inner wall of your back. When you slump, they swing forward and are subject to fatiguing vibration and possible damage.

As one instructor put it, "If riding produces a backache or a desire to stop at every rest station and places in between, then you are probably giving your kidneys a beating through poor riding posture. Straighten up, and unless there is something organically wrong, your trouble will go away."

Keep It Pegged

Equally important in sitting a bike is to keep one's feet on the pegs. A dragging toe can easily catch on a road obstruction. Also, the rear brake and shift pedals are placed so they can be instantly applied. But this can be done only if the rider's feet are in the correct position.

Importance of the Dry Run

Instructors vary in their approach to teaching a novice how to ride, but they are all in agreement on the importance of dry runs before the beginner actually takes his first real ride. They also agree that just a quick run-through is insufficient. It is necessary for the beginner to drill himself until he knows thoroughly the operation and position of every control.

Although it is hard for an impatient novice to hold back, some instructors refuse to let their students ride a bike the first day. The instruction is all drill and more drill. Then when the student thoroughly understands his machine, he is given his first opportunity to get it moving.

Actually this isn't as bad as the beginner might think. There isn't too much to learn about a cycle and it can be learned quickly. Some say they can learn it all in an hour. However, learning how to use the controls and getting sufficient practice so that reaction is automatic is something else. This r juires a lot of repetition.

Quicker Than Auto Instruction

Those impatient with this highly desirable dry running should think back over the time it took for them to learn to drive a car. Most driving schools take a minimum of from eight to ten sessions. It is not unreasonable, then, to devote one day to practicing the controls of a motorcycle.

This basic instruction can be summed up in this way:

- Learn the bike's nomenclature so you can name the major parts.
- Learn now to use the throttle.
- Learn how the clutch works and how to coordinate the throttle and clutch.
- Learn how to use the front-wheel and back-wheel brakes.
- Learn to sit the saddle correctly.
- Finally, learn how to start the engine safely.
- This, of course, is not all there is to it. Many things you must learn cannot be taught from a stopped cycle. They must be taught from a bike in motion.

So—let's get moving!

Chapter 3

MOVING ON

You begin your first real ride with a "straight-line drive." That is, we won't worry about turning and cornering at this point. We will be satisfied with just moving straight ahead.

Unless a beginner has had experience riding bicycles and knows how to balance a two-wheel vehicle, it is better to begin practice away from the pavement or roadway. A grassy lot or field is ideal. An area with loose gravel and dirt is best avoided. In such a location a slip or fall won't tear your hide.

Starting Procedure

The first thing to learn is to balance. You can do this by having someone push you before you start the engine. Then you stop and start the engine in this manner.

- Insure that gearshift is in neutral.
- Open the cutoff valve between tank and carburetor.
- If engine is cold, move choke lever (on carburetor) to the fully prime position (all the way down).

33

- Open the throttle by rotating the handgrip one-quarter turn, BUT DO NOT TURN ON THE IGNITION.
- Now kick down on the starter pedal two times to prime the cylinders. Priming the cylinders means that we are filling them with a full charge of air-gas mixture from the carburetor.
- After priming the cylinders, move the choke lever up to one-quarter closed position. Then set the spark control (by rotating the left-hand grip) one-quarter advanced.
- Keep throttle at one-quarter opening and turn on the ignition key. Both hands should be on the handlebar grips controlling the throttle and spark.
- Now kick down vigorously on the kick-starter pedal, observing the safety precautions enumerated earlier.
- When the engine starts, advance spark and open throttle just enough to keep engine idling properly. When the engine has warmed, pull the choke control to the top position.

Easy Does It

Now with the engine running and the jiffy stand or wheel stand (whichever the case may be) in the up position, it is easy to see why motorcycles have so many controls hand-operated. One foot is necessary to keep the machine upright. The second foot is needed for the gearshift pedal. So, unlike the automobile, the throttle and clutch must be hand-operated.

The secret of a smooth start is the ability to open the throttle properly while smoothly engaging the clutch. Otherwise we face the same problem that a beginner encounters in an automobile. Too little gas will cause

In proper riding position both feet are close to the foot controls. In the above picture, the left foot (as seen by the viewer, but actually the rider's right foot) is right over the gearshift lever, while the other foot is in a position to shift over on the rear-brake lever at a second's notice.

both vehicles to stall, while too much—accompanied by a jerky clutch release—will cause the vehicles to jump, jerk, and perhaps die.

There is an extra hazard in applying too much starting power with a cycle that one doesn't face in a car. More than a few beginners over the years have revved up the engine too high, squeezed the clutch lever, slammed the gearshift pedal down into low, and released the clutch— then sat down hard on the ground while their mechanical mount started off by itself.

Hug with the Knees

The best way to start is to lean slight forward and press your knees against the gas tank as insurance against being thrown off balance by a too sudden start.

A major danger of a too-sudden start is that the novice

may unconsciously twist the throttle grip in trying to keep his balance. This could easily send him plowing into the rear of someone ahead or even dump him in the street.

The throttle control works through a cable that extends from the grip to the carburetor. Interior designs of carburetors vary with different manufacturers. However, one common design has a throttle slide that raises and lowers a needle valve into the carb main jet to decrease or increase the flow of gasoline.

The Sticking Throttle

Despite the usually free working of such devices, throttles do stick occasionally, just as they do on automobiles. It is quite a shock to the average beginner the first time he is faced with a sticking throttle. Sometimes, of course, a runaway engine is not a true throttle stick; it is just that the beginner has forgotten how to use the throttle. The effect is the same. The engine is going faster than the rider desires.

When this happens there is no cause for panic. You simply disengage the clutch by squeezing on the clutch-control lever. This disconnects the power to your back wheel. Then you can coast and brake to a stop, cutting the ignition off after you stop.

Note that it isn't a good idea to cut the ignition *before* you stop. You might find yourself in a traffic emergency where you need control of your cycle, and you will not have it with a dead engine.

It is a very good idea to drill into your mind that *turning the grip outward slows down the engine.*

Starting Out

For your first real ride it is well to make the entire short run in low gear. Generally a first rider has enough to think about without having to shift as well. This first ride should not be long. It should be just enough to give you the feel of the machine in motion, to determine if you can balance it satisfactorily, and to give you the feel of the throttle, clutch, and brake.

The initial slow speed in low will give you good practice without the danger of taking a spill. More often than not a beginner hits his brakes too hard the first few times.

If you negotiate the first straight line satisfactorily, then it is time to move up in speed. This time make the same run, shifting to second, and then to high.

Here is a summary of the complete procedure as a review.

- Start the machine with the gear in neutral. Release the clutch and shift into low by depressing the gearshift pedal. Increase power by evenly turning the throttle grip toward you and just as evenly release your grip on the clutch control lever. You should now be under way.
- If the cycle jerks a little, that isn't bad for a beginning if things smooth out immediately. If the lugging ("clanking" at low speeds) is too rough or if you kill the engine, put the gears back in neutral and start all over again.
- If your start is O.K., release the clutch, slack off on the throttle slightly, and lift the shift lever with your toe to shift to second.

- Now, as you pick up speed, you can again toe the shift lever up to shift to high. Or if you are still unsure of yourself, you can practice only shifting into second until you become more proficient in coordinating clutch and pedal gear.

- To stop, close the throttle by turning it *away* from you, reducing the speed to idle, and release the clutch. Brake by using the rear-wheel brake (foot pedal). Apply the rear-wheel brake first and then, as the machine slows, squeeze in slowly on the front-wheel brake lever. Put out your foot to balance the machine when it stops so that you and it will not fall over. Shift down to neutral, for you should never leave the cycle in gear when it is stopped. If your hand should slip on the clutch lever, your mount could jump out from under you.

Do It Again

Simple test runs on a straight line should be repeated, using every gear, until you can shift easily and can smoothly coordinate the actions of clutch and gear. Frequent stops should be made to get practice in starting and stopping, shifting up and down, and in returning the gears to neutral.

You'll learn to ride better if you don't try to do too much at once. Start with basic procedures and then gradually add other operations as you learn. Now after you have learned to ride a straight course satisfactorily, it is time to learn to *turn* your cycle.

At normal speed it is only necessary to lean in the direction you wish to turn. As if it were part of you, the cycle follows your motions. At slow speeds, however, it will be necessary for you to turn the handlebars as well as lean. Three-wheel cycles also must be turned with the handlebars, as must cycles equipped with sidecars.

How Leaning Causes Bikes to Turn

A question that often puzzles beginners is why motorcycles can be turned around a corner simply by leaning the body in the desired direction.

A motorcycle is governed by the law of inertia. In physics this is the law that if a body is at rest it will remain at rest or if in motion will continue moving unless acted on by an outside force. An example is the planets in their orbits. Once placed in motion about the sun they will continue moving until something forces them to stop or changes their direction.

Under this physical law, a motorcycle once started moving in a straight line will continue moving in a straight line unless something acts to change the direction.

Also the wheels, chains, flywheel, and crankshaft of

Turning, except at very slow speeds, is done by leaning your body in the direction you wish to turn. The degree of turn is controlled by how much you lean and how fast you are going. At very slow speeds, you will have to steer with the handlebars also.

the engine rotate in the same plane that the motorcycle is traveling and at right angles to the ground. This acts as a gyroscopic action to help maintain upright stability of the cycle as long as it is moving at a sufficient rate of speed to overcome the pull of gravity. The higher the rate of a cycle's speed, the harder inertia and gyroscopic action will work to keep it upright and moving.

When you lean on a moving motorcycle, your body supplies the outside force which, according to the law of inertia in physics, is necessary to change the tendency of the body (the cycle) to keep moving in the direction that it was started.

How Much to Lean

How much to lean is something that a rider must learn through intensive practice. The amount of directional lean will vary with speed and the radius of the curve you are traveling.

If you don't lean far enough, you will either run off the road on the opposite side of your turn or, at least, curve over into the opposing lane of traffic. Either mistake can be disastrous.

On the other hand, if you lean too far, you may lay the machine over on its side for a hide-removing skid.

The only thing to do is practice on a vacant lot until you get the feel of the lean at different speeds. This is not difficult to learn and is a lot of fun in itself. One instructor recommends scattering pasteboard boxes around your vacant lot and weaving your course through them. If you make a mistake and run over one, you haven't hurt either yourself or your motorcycle. And the practice will do wonders for your riding technique.

Eventually you will get to the point where you will

automatically select the right degree of lean for any given speed.

What Keeps It Up?

A frequent question of the unitiated is, "What keeps the cycle from falling over when you lean out so far on these fast turns and curves?"

The sad truth is that cycles don't *always* stay up on sharp curves. When they do slip, it is always the rider's fault—unless the accident was caused by a bolt of lightning or other act of God. A correctly handled motorcycle, ridden by a rider who understands his mount and watches for road hazards, will always negotiate a turn or curve without skidding.

When any type of vehicle—whether motorcycle, plane or car—turns swiftly, centrifugal force tends to push the vehicle away from the center of the circle it is turning. You can feel this force as it tends to throw you against the opposite side of a car that is making a fast turn.

When you lean into a turn in traveling a curve on a motorcycle, the leaning of your body—that is, the shift of your weight—balances the centrifugal force that is trying to push the cycle away from the turn.

The greater the centrifugal force generated by your speed, the more you can lean before your body upsets the stability of the cycle. Stability in a curve, then, is dependent upon how far you lean, which in turn is dependent upon how fast you are going.

Your Tires Help

An examination of the tires on your new bike will show that they differ quite a bit from those on an automobile. The tread on a car's tires is more flat so that the rubber will grip the road, giving good traction. A motorcycle needs traction too. However, the constant need to lean the cycle over to make turns requires a tire that wraps the tread farther up the sides of the casing. They have been built this way to insure that the tread will contact the road during turns. This tread is additional insurance against having the cycle slip out from under you when you bank for a turn.

There is a lot of misunderstanding about tire treads. Tire experts tell us—contrary to what a lot of drivers think —that a smooth, treadless tire will stop a vehicle just as fast as a tire with tread (that is, grooves cut in the rubber) *on a dry pavement.*

Unfortunately all our driving is not on such a smooth surface. Grooves in the tires serve a double purpose. By flexing and compressing, they allow small areas of the tire to act independently and provide greater traction on uneven surfaces. But it is on wet pavement that grooved treads are most important. On wet surfaces the smooth tire that grips well ordinarily will skid dangerously. The grooves on regular tires act as a water squeegee to sweep the water away and permit the tire to get a surer grip.

In somewhat the same manner, an entirely different tire is necessary for very soft ground, such as sand. Here you will find the "knobby" tires a distinct advantage. Such tires have very coarse tread that look like knobs of rubber which dig down into the loose ground and give firmer traction. We'll take a closer look at them when we get around to trail riding a little later.

Slipping the Clutch

Before we leave our vacant-lot practice field and move out on the streets and highways, there is an essential driving procedure we have to learn. This is called "slipping the clutch," previously referred to in Chapter 2.

First, let's consider what happens to the power generated in our motorcycle engine. A gas-air mixture burned in the cylinder puts pressure on the piston. This pressure is transferred through the connecting rod to the crankshaft, causing the crankshaft to turn. This action transfers and changes our up-and-down force to rotary force or torque. Torque is defined as a "twisting force." The crankshaft force turns the flywheel, the gears, and the sprocket wheel. The drive chain transfers the power from the smaller sprocket gear to the larger sprocket gear on the back wheel of the cycle to deliver power to drive the machine. Some means is necessary to stop this power flow without stopping the engine. This is done by the clutch.

As we have learned earlier, the clutch is disengaged by squeezing the clutch-control lever on the handlebar. However, the actual clutch itself is a series of discs which strong springs press tightly against the flywheel. When the clutch is disengaged, the discs are pulled back from the flywheel so that no contact is made. When engaged, the clutch literally "clutches" the flywheel so tightly that it revolves with the flywheel without slipping.

The clutch in an automobile and the clutch in a motorcycle work in a similar manner, although their construction is different. One of the differences is the number of discs in the clutch assembly. The automobile clutch has a single disc, whereas the motorcycle clutch has as many as six friction discs in its assembly.

A Stronger Clutch

A slipping clutch is one that does not firmly engage the flywheel. The clutch disc, instead of revolving the same number of times as the flywheel, slips to a varying degree. This does not permit the full power of the engine to be transmitted to the final drive.

Slipping the clutch in an automobile, with its single friction disc, will quickly burn out the clutch. This ruins the clutch and requires an expensive overhaul job. The motorcycle clutch, with its multidiscs, spreads the friction over much more area.

These multiple discs in the clutch permits a rider to slip his motorcycle clutch without fear of immediately burning out the friction discs. There is no denying that slipping a clutch does wear it out faster and it also prevents full power from getting to the final drive.

Then why do it?

Here is the answer. At best an internal combustion engine is a jerky operation. It operates through a series of bangs. The fuel mixture ignites and bangs the piston down. The crankshaft pushes the piston up again and another bang drives the piston down still another time.

If there are enough of these bangs and they are properly spaced in between each other, the engine will run smoothly. This is what happens in four-, six-, and eight-cylinder automobiles. But while there are some four-cylinder motorcycles, the majority have only one or two cylinders. Such engines run smoothly at higher revolutions where the bangs come close together.

At slow speeds, the bangs are spaced farther apart and when the clutch is fully engaged, you can feel every power stroke. At these low speeds, the cycle may start to jerk and clank the rear chain. This is known as "lugging."

Solving the Lugging Problem

Lugging is what happens in an automobile when you try to go up a too steep hill in high. Speed falls off. The motor starts to jerk and will stop unless you shift to a lower gear with additional power.

The answer to lugging in a motorcycle is the same as in a car. You shift to a lower gear. This works very well when the cycle is under a heavy load, such as climbing a grade, pulling a weighty burden, or reducing speed.

However, in very slow traffic it is not always possible to gear a motorcycle low enough that it will be able to

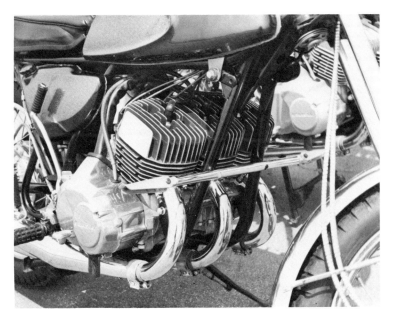

Multiengine cycles have less tendency to "lug" at low speeds. In addition they provide greater power which is appreciated by racers and long road runners. This is a three-cylinder Kawasaki.

keep its engine revolutions high enough to prevent lugging.

Two-cylinder engines do better than one-cylinder engines because you have twice the number of bangs per revolution. But there is a limit to how slow you can run either the one- or two-bangers without lugging.

If you try to inch along below this speed, the cycle will begin to jerk, putting a strain on the power train and particularly on the drive chain to the rear wheel. The problem is complicated because at this slow speed it is difficult for even an experienced rider to hold a constant low speed with his hand throttle.

So when it is not possible to gear down so that you can keep your engine revolutions high enough to prevent lugging, you solve your problem by slipping the clutch.

How to Slip the Clutch

The clutch is slipped by *partially* disengaging the clutch by depressing the clutch lever a small amount with your left hand. Full depression, of course, completely disengages the clutch. You select a steady rpm (revolution per minute) that will keep you going in the lowest gear without lugging. Then you cut down on the power to the drive train by slipping the clutch just enough to reduce the speed of the machine without reducing the speed or rpms of the engine. This may call for a constant readjustment of the clutch pressure through the hand clutch control lever.

Slipping the clutch is a technique you will find very valuable in extremely heavy traffic or when riding in formation such as parades or club shows. However, it should never be done except when necessary, because heat and friction are the inevitable result of slipping clutches. Prolonged use will lead to trouble, although not as quickly as in a motor car.

On the streets and highways when speed will permit, it is best to kick down into a lower gear rather than slip the clutch in high or second.

Practice Clutch Slipping

Most instructors recommend that practice clutch slipping be done with the machine on a rear stand rather than actually running on the practice field. This provides better control. However, if this is done, the practice sessions should be as short as possible. You must put on the brake to provide the resistance so the engine will react. This means you will be heating up the brakes, the clutch, and the engine. Keep it up too long and you're in trouble. It should be noted here that a motorcycle engine is air-cooled and is designed for maximum efficiency while moving. While the engine will idle satisfactorily, revving up the motor too high will cause overheating.

Once you have mastered the controls, have proven your ability to shift and to use the clutch and brake properly, then you are ready for your first ride off the practice field and out into the streets. Here you will face new problems—natural road hazards, and the greatest driving hazard of them all. Your fellow drivers.

Chapter 4

ON THE STREET

One of the first things that a new rider must remember when he takes his bike off private property for the first time and rolls out in the city streets is that he is riding a *motor vehicle.*

This may seem elementary, but many don't seem to realize it. Laws that govern traffic on the public highways are not *automobile* laws solely. *They are motor vehicle laws.* They apply to all vehicles from huge trucks to motorcycles.

This means that in order to ride on the streets and highways you must understand and abide by the vehicle code of your individual states. This involves following not only the general vehicle laws but also the extra ones passed just for the benefit of cyclists. Since traffic is both a state and a municipality problem, laws vary from state to state and even from town to town within states.

You will need a driver's license. Here again the requirements differ among states. As an example, California re-

48

quires a motorcycle rider to hold a regular driver's license and then have it endorsed for motorcycle riding after an additional written examination and a driving examination.

The written examination covers special state motorcycle regulations, motorcycle safety rules, and proper equipment. Many of these are different from those of cars by the very nature of the two vehicles. For example, a puddle of oil that would never pose a threat to a car is sufficient to put a cycle into a deadly skid.

Here are California's Motorcycle Regulations as put forth in the special supplement to the Driver's Handbook issued by the California Department of Motor Vehicles. While these rules may not be exactly the same as those in effect in other states, if you comply with them you are on safe gound in any state.

Freeways

Motor-driven cycles (motorcycles having less than 15 gross brake horsepower) are not permitted on the freeways, which are posted to give notice of such prohibition. [This means light cycles and mini-bikes of roughly less than 125 cc displacement.] This law is to insure that cycles can travel fast enough to keep with the normal traffic flow on freeways. Riding a motor scooter in fast freeway traffic is an invitation to disaster.

Passengers

You may not carry a passenger on a motorcycle except on a seat securely fastened to the machine in the rear of the driver and provided with footrests, or in a sidecar attached to the motorcycle. This sidecar must be designed for a passenger. Any passenger is required to keep his feet on the footrests while the motorcycle is in motion.

Parking

When parking your motorcycle at the curb, at least one wheel or fender must be touching the curb. Be on the alert for city ordinances which require special parking rules for motorcycles.

Equipment Regulations

Mirrors

Every motorcycle must be equipped with a mirror so located as to reflect to the driver a view of the highway for a distance of at least 200 feet to the rear.

Windshields

When a windshield is used on a motorcycle manufactured after Jan. 1, 1969, the material must be "safety" glazing material. [Glazing, in this case, would refer to any type of transparent material used in the windshield, either plastic or glass.]

Seats

The seat on a two-wheel motorcycle must be positioned so that the driver, when sitting astride the seat, can reach the ground with his feet.

Handlebars

Handlebars may not be more than 15 inches in height above that portion of the seat occupied by the rider when occupied and depressed by his weight. [This outlaws the "ape-hangers" or extremely high handlebars which are tiring to ride and more difficult to control.]

Brakes

Motorcycles must have service brakes on all wheels, except that motorcycles manufactured prior to 1966 need have brakes on only one wheel. The brakes must be capable of stopping the motorcycle within 25 feet from a speed of 20 miles per hour.

Headlamps

Every motorcycle must be equipped with at least one and not more than two lighted headlamps when operated during darkness. The headlamp on a motor-driven cycle may be of the single-beam or multiple-beam type but must conform to the following regulations:

(a) It must be of sufficient intensity to reveal a person or a vehicle at a distance of not less than 100 feet when the cycle is operated at speeds less than 25 miles per hour, and not less than 200 feet at speeds from 25 to 35 miles per hour, and not less than 300 feet at speeds exceeding 35 miles per hour.

(b) If a multiple-beam headlamp is used, the upper beam must meet all of the above requirements and the lower beam must be of sufficient intensity to reveal a person or a vehicle at a distance of not less than 100 feet.

(c) If a single-beam headlamp is used, it must be so aimed that when the cycle is loaded none of the high-intensity portion of the light, at a distance of 25 feet ahead, projects higher than the level of the center of the lamp from which it comes.

The Written Examination

Many of these regulations and rules may be checked by the examiner when giving you your driving examination, or they may be included in the written exam.

The written examination will be along the same line and style as the one you were required to take for a regular driver's license. However, the questions will be slanted toward the peculiar safety problems of the motorcycle rider. Questions are changed periodically, but below are a few examples of those sometimes used. They are included here just to give you an idea of what to expect. From your state highway department you should be able to obtain pamphlets covering the points that may be included in driver's tests in your own state.

"When making an emergency stop with a locked rear wheel, how do you aim your front wheel?" The answer would be to keep the front wheel aimed directly ahead. You do not try to correct for the side-to-side swerve of the rear wheel by turning your front wheel.

Another question often encountered is, "When is it permissible to pass between the curb lane traffic and the curb?" The answer here is NEVER! Passing on the right between a car and the curb is extremely dangerous, for you may be caught by a car that is intending to turn, park, or enter a driveway.

Still another is, "If you encounter unavoidable bumps or obstacles in the road, how should you ride over them?'' The answer would be to hit them at right angles. In this way the tire would have a tendency to ride straight over the bump. If you hit at an angle, there is more danger of throwing the cycle into a swerve or even upsetting yourself.

State laws also vary as to the minimum age for a driver's license. In California it is sixteen with parental consent. Since the United States Constitution requires each state to respect the laws of the others, drivers may use their out-of-state licenses on trips to other states if the vehicle is registered in the same state that granted the driver's license. However, if a driver takes permanent residence in the new state, he is required to obtain that state's driver's license.

There are some gimmicks attached to many of these ''reciprocity laws.'' California, for example, requires non-resident drivers *under 21* to obtain a ''certificate of compliance'' within ten days of entering the state as a licensed driver. This certificate is to show proof that the driver can be responsible for damages in case of accidents. In other words, you must prove that you have public liability insurance.

The question of liability insurance is a tricky one at the present time, because of a recent decision of the U.S. Supreme Court. Some states have compulsory public liability insurance laws. Others do not make liability insurance mandatory but require drivers who are involved in accidents to furnish ''proof of responsibility to respond to damages'' or have their driving licenses revoked.

Under the latter laws, if you are involved in an accident —even though you may not have been at fault—you must either show that you do have liability insurance or post a bond up to $25,000 in order to keep your driving privilege in that state.

The Supreme Court decision mentioned above answered an Iowa minister whose license had been revoked under such a law. The court ruled that states could not *revoke* licenses under such laws. However, the court went on to say that it was constitutional for states to have mandatory insurance laws as a prerequisite to getting a license in the first place.

As a result of this decision, it is expected that states may change their laws to require mandatory insurance.

Assigned Risk Insurance

What happens to so-called "poor risk" drivers in states requiring mandatory insurance? Insurance companies don't want to insure them and the state demands it. In such cases there is usually an "assigned risk" law. The state requires insurance companies in its jurisdiction to pool the risks. They must divide up the poor risks and insure them. However, the rates are often exorbitant.

Another question that comes up with beginners is "What clothing should a rider wear?" Well, this seems to be a question no two have the same answer for. Doug Berger, president of the Southern California Motorcycle Association, in a safety pamphlet he wrote for his members, recommends a helmet as a minimum and adds, "You should not ride a bike while dressed for the beach any more than you should swim in riding clothes. Any bike can go down. So if you want to be prudent it is best to wear clothing that will afford you the best protection. Leather jackets, shirts and pants and good gauntlet gloves will do the job best of helping you not to pave the road with your hide."

In some states wearing approved helmets is mandatory. California does not have a mandatory helmet law.

If your bike does not have a windshield, a helmet with a shatterproof plastic face shield is a tremendous help. If you don't wear it, a pair of goggles or wraparound sun glasses—again with shatterproof lenses of the industrial type—are a great help.

Once, heavy goggles were an indispensable part of a motorcyclist's equipment. But this was in the days of poor roads where one plowed through clouds of dirt and dust on every ride. Today goggles aren't seen much anymore. This is a pity. Just recall the number of bugs that smash against your automobile windshield in the summer. It just takes one of those in your eye to cause real trouble.

Emergency Stops

There is one last caution that you should prepare for before finally taking your bike onto the city streets for the first time. This is a careful drill in making an emergency stop.

Previously you learned that a motorcycle has both a rear and a front brake and that the two are operated independently. The rear-wheel brake is operated by a foot pedal, which may be on either side of the engine (depending upon the manufacturer) but is always on the side opposite the clutch pedal. The front-wheel brake is hand-operated by a lever on the handlebar. Hand controls are more uniform. The brake control is on the right and is operated by the fingers of the right hand.

The two brakes behave quite differently in operation and pose individual problems in emergency braking.

There is a definite technique to be learned. To do this we must consider each of the brakes individually.

In general brakes can be divided into two main types, both operating by applying friction against the wheels to slow down their revolutions. The best-known type is the expanding shoe brake. Here "shoes" inside the brake drum are expanded by pressure from the operating cable which causes the shoes to rub against the inside of the brake drum. Shoes are covered with a brake lining as a buffer between the two metal parts.

The second type of brake is the disc brake, which is just beginning to appear on some models of motorcycles. Here the brake drum is replaced by a metal disc. The brake consists of a cantilever clamp, which grips both sides of the disc, giving greater stopping power in addition to other advantages.

The Rear-Wheel Brake

We will first consider the rear-wheel brake, because it is the one you apply first. The rear wheel can be locked by depressing the brake lever all the way. When this happens the wheel will not necessarily skid forward, as happens when a car's rear wheels are locked. The rear wheels may "fishtail" or skid from side to side. Or the bike may go into a broadslide—which is a sidewise skid at right angles to the direction of travel.

The possibility of broadsliding is increased if weight on the cycle—either the driver's or a load he may be carrying—is not evenly balanced, or if the road is sloping, or if there is uneven wear on the tires. This can also happen if the rider is forced to turn his front wheel to miss an obstacle at the same time he locks his back wheels.

Broadsliding always gives a beginner a sinking feeling in the pit of his stomach the first time it occurs. But experienced riders insist that it is not particularly dangerous. They say that if you hold your front wheel straight in the line of travel regardless of what the rear end wants to do, you'll come out of the skid all right.

If the front wheel is kept straight in the original line of travel—that is, pointed straight down the road—you can come out of the skid simply by letting up on the brake. The natural stability of the machine will pull you right into line. This, of course, applies only when the back wheel is skidding because of brake lock. If both wheels are skidding, then you have a different situation.

Incidently, if you are traveling at a high rate of speed, you should release the rear brake gradually to pull out of your broadslide skid. Otherwise, you could get a whip action that could upset you entirely.

The Front-Wheel Brake

The front-wheel brake operates, as we have previously noted, from the right-hand lever. The brake—unlike the rear one—is so constructed that it will not lock on any road that has good traction. This is done by designing the brake so that the friction between the road and the tire is greater than the friction between the brake and the brake drum.

However, if the road is slippery or covered with loose dirt or gravel, this condition could cause the tire to lose traction. In such cases, the brake-drum friction may become greater than the road friction. Then the front-wheel brake can lock.

When the back-wheel brake locks, you still can control

Disc brakes are now beginning to appear on motorcycles. This front wheel, double-disc set was seen on a new Honda.

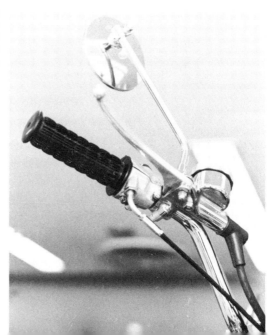

The front wheel of this Honda features a double shoe brake. The brake cable is the lower of the two cables snaking upward. The top cable operates the speedometer.

Front-wheel brake lever on the Norton 750-cc motorcycle. Note rear-view mirror attached to the handlebar. This is a required safety accessory in most states.

your machine, but if the front-wheel brake locks you lose control. As one experienced rider put it, "then you look for a soft spot to land on."

You can avoid this difficult by relying on your rear brake on slippery or loose surfaces.

You Still Need Both

This does not mean that you should neglect your front brake. A good driver will use his front brake more than he does his rear one.

You will notice that the rider sits more to the back of a cycle. This puts more of his weight on the back wheels. But then when the brakes began to bite into the speed, this weight is shifted toward the front. Remember how in a car you almost slam into the windshield when the driver hits hard on his brakes. This decreases the load on the back wheel and increases the load on the front wheel. A manual put out by the makers of the Suzuki motorcycle estimates that 70 percent of your stopping capacity thus shifts from your back-wheel brake to your front-wheel brake.

The weight shift gives the front brake an increasingly greater share of the motorcycle's grip on the roadway, which also gives it greater braking ability. This means that your front brake is very important and should be your best means of stopping at cruising speeds.

The front brake is more sensitive and its use can affect your steering. As noted earlier, it is dangerous to use in traction-poor situations. At slow speeds, where the weight transfer is so much less, the rear brake is more effective than the front brake.

So it can be seen that both brakes have their advantages. In actual practice, good riders don't choose between them, but use both to stop smoothly, correctly, and safely. As a team the two brakes give you maximum stopping power.

Take It Easy on the Brakes

The basic rule for braking is to take it as easy as possible. You are well advised to do the same thing a good driver does in an automobile. This is to let your engine do most of your braking for you, which is accomplished by down-shifting. That is, you go to the next lower gear so that the compression of your engine slows you down.

On a motorcycle, if you anticipate your stops, down-shift to slow down, and then apply first your rear brake and then your front brake, you'll come to a safe, easy stop with a minimum of wear on your brakes.

Occasionally, however, you may find it necessary to stop in a real hurry. The procedure for emergency stops, as given by the California Highway Patrol Academy to its motorcycle students, is this:

- Apply rear-wheel brake, locking rear wheel.
- Close throttle, cutting off gas supply, and release clutch.
- At the same time, apply front-wheel brake, but keep front wheel straight with the direction of travel.
- If the machine broadslides, hold wheel straight with the direction of travel and hold balance by leaning *away* from side to which rear-end is sliding.

Broadsliding is not dangerous, as we noted earlier. It is an accepted motorcycling technique in racing. However, it is important that it be done deliberately only where there is room to slide sideways. On a highway you may be boxed in between traffic so that a sideways slide could throw you into the other lane, with disastrous results.

What we are trying to say here is that there is no rule or technique that is correct for every situation, except the rule "Never fail to expect the unexpected."

Chapter 5

HAZARDS OF
STREET AND HIGHWAY

When you take your first motorcycle off the training field and into the street, you are entering the world's biggest obstacle course. Ordinarily if someone claims that the whole world is against him, you had best refer the individual to a psychiatrist—unless the speaker happens to be a motorcycle rider. In that case he just may be right.

The sad fact is that the death rate per 100 million vehicle miles is four times higher for motorcycle riders than for automobile drivers. However, this does not mean that motorcycles in themselves are four times as dangerous as automobiles. The Automobile Club of Southern California, an affiliate of AAA—the Automobile Association of America—is authority for the figure that the motorcycle driver is at fault only 39 percent of the time in collisions between automobiles and motorcycles.

It would appear then that the automobile and its driver are among the motorcyclists' worst enemies. Since car drivers aren't getting any better, the burden in the car-versus-motorcycle fight must be carried by the cyclist.

Car versus Cycle

Unless you are willing to restrict your motorcycling to desert runs, trail driving, or racing on closed tracks, automobiles are a way of life that you will just have to get used to. It is not that automobile drivers are particularly vicious and have declared a vendetta against motorcyclists (although I know a number of cyclists who believe that motorists as a class are in fact waging an undeclared war on them. It is just that the peculiarities of cars and cycles make them natural enemies.

In the first place, a motorcycle is small and has a low silhouette. An automobile naturally has two blind spots on each side where it is difficult to see passing vehicles. It is the area between the view given by your automobile rear-view mirror and the area you can see ahead of you. Not even the addition of a side mirror can completely cover this blind area.

If you have ever taken a road test for an automobile drivers' license, you probably failed the examination if you did not turn your head to check these blind spots before changing lanes.

The small size of a motorcycle often causes it to be overlooked by drivers checking their blind spots. Also, in fast-moving traffic, a driver has only an opportunity to glance back quickly for he must get his sight back on the road ahead of him. A fast-moving cycle can easily move into the blind spot as the car driver turns his attention back to the highway ahead. The result is that the car may cut directly in front of the oncoming motorcycle.

Defensive Driving

In such an event, the best the motorcycle rider can hope for is an emergency stop. The worst that can happen is a smashup that may be fatal.

We are assuming here that the car driver has followed the principles of safe driving and checked before changing lanes. Many don't. And that complicates motorcycling in traffic still further. This is no academic problem thought up by instructors to frighten students. It is a serious condition, as any experienced motorcyclist will tell you. As one put it, "Cars aren't afraid of cycles. They'll see you approaching an intersection in the opposing lane, but will cut in front of you to make their left turn in violation of all rules of safety. They would never do that with a big truck and probably not with another car, for they know these big boys can't stop fast. But they seem to think that they can make it in front of a cycle, or that they can bluff the cyclist into slowing down."

Fortunately for the future of motorcycling—and the future of those who motorcycle, especially—there is something you can do about this very poor situation: Drive defensively.

Driving defensively means simply keeping alert, watching for hazards of the road, and assuming the worst of your fellow drivers. It also means "driving ahead of yourself." Some instructors will advise you to drive as much as a city block (200 feet) in front of your cycle. By this they mean to watch the traffic that far ahead, instead of just paying attention to the car in front of you.

Anticipate the Action

In this way you can anticipate what the immediate car in front of you might do. When you see taillights flare up a block ahead, you know that the gent in front of you will be slamming on his brakes as soon as the thought impulse travels from his mind to his left leg. You'll be that much ahead if you start braking the same time he does instead of waiting until you see the red of his tail. Otherwise you'll have to add your own reaction time after he begins braking instead of reacting along with him.

According to safety experts who figure out these things, at a speed of 20 miles per hour your cycle will travel 20 feet while you're thinking about hitting the brake and then will roll another 20 feet before you can stop the wheels from turning. At a speed of 30 mph, it will require 75 feet to stop, and at 50 mph you will use up 175 feet before you can drop your feet to the pavement under the most favorable conditions.

So you can see where the extra margin gained by "driving ahead" of the car in front of you pays off in giving you a head start on that gentleman, possibly preventing his rear end from becoming your crash pad if he stops suddenly and you don't.

Too, there is always the possibility that the car in front of you might not realize his danger at all. Drivers have a way of fiddling with the radio or air conditioner, watching the girls go by, or thinking about pleasures and problems as they drive along. If you wait for his taillight to warn you of danger ahead, it may be too late.

Riding the Line

Once we've agreed that motorcycling safety in traffic depends upon keeping an eye on the cars ahead of the one we are following, then it becomes apparent that we must revise a standard driving technique. Many of the rules of safe driving apply equally well to cars or motorbikes. But the rule that you should stay in the center of your lane, while great for cars, is poor motorcycle technique.

Staying in the center of the lane provides a car driver with the maximum clearance between himself and the cars in the lanes on each side of him. But if a motorcycle keeps to the center, directly between the two white lines, his forward vision will be completely obscured by the car in front of him.

The cyclist is in as bad a spot as a motorist stuck behind a slow-moving truck or trailer. He can't see anything but the rear end of the truck. Any trouble that may suddenly develop ahead, any dips or obstructions or sudden curves, will be masked from the cyclist's sight.

So instead of riding in the middle of the lane, motorcycle riders are advised to move over close to the dividing line between the traffic lanes.

Remember this is *close* to the line—not *on* it or *over* it. In effect this puts your vision between the lanes of traffic, permitting you to see farther down the road or street.

Some unthinking cyclists take advantage of this increased view to shorten the distance between themselves and the car ahead. They feel that if something happens, like the car's stopping suddenly, they can simply scoot right on through the gap between the car in front and the car in the lane beside it.

This is like putting a second cartridge in the chamber for your Russian roulette game of the highway.

Beware the Gap

Depending on the gap between the lanes of traffic as an escape hatch is bad, but using it as a means of moving faster than the flow of traffic is worse.

You have absolutely no way of knowing when that inviting gap will suddenly close in, trapping you between the cars on your right and left. Remember that when you zip through the gap like this you are coming right out of the blind spots of both cars between which you are trying to squeeze. The only possible way that either driver can know you are coming is to turn his head and look for you. He has no reason to do so. In fact he may suddenly decide to swerve slightly to avoid a road obstruction or just to check the line of traffic ahead. He is in his lane and perfectly within his rights.

Motorcycle-scooting between slower-moving lanes of traffic is very prevalent on freeways during rush hours. States appear to be very lax about stopping this dangerous practice. California, for example, has no law prohibiting it.

Recently an indignant woman driver wrote an angry letter to a Los Angeles newspaper. She claimed she was so badly frightened by the sudden appearance of a motorcyclist between her and a car in the adjoining lane that she almost swerved into the car passing on the opposite lane. She wanted to know if something couldn't be done about the practice.

After a check with the Highway Patrol, the newspaper replied that the practice was not forbidden by law. The car, being ahead, had the legal right of way. So if anything did happen, the cyclist would be considered at fault. Knowledge that the cyclist was at fault is rather poor consolation when your next ride is in an ambulance or hearse.

How to Pass Safely

The first rule in passing safely is to be sure there is a reason for passing. A lane-changer who swings constantly from one lane to another as he seeks to weave his way ahead of traffic is a traffic hazard himself. In most cases you are better off moving with the flow of traffic than trying always to keep ahead of the pack.

The second rule is to insure that the way is clear and that you have the right of way. You always pass on the left side of the car you are going around—that is, on the driver's side. The only exception to this rule is when you are traveling on a multilane highway or street. Then you can swing into the right lane and pass. After assuring yourself that the way is clear in front, you check your rear-view mirror and glance back over your shoulder to insure that no car or other cycle is moving in your blind spot.

You should assure yourself that the lane left of the car you wish to pass is also clear. This avoids forcing you to ride a gap between the two with the dangers noted earlier.

It is also well not to try to pass when another car is moving parallel with the one you wish to pass, even though your full passing lane is open between them. There have been many wrecks because two parallel cars have both decided to move into the lane between them at the same time.

Then you move out into the passing lane, swinging out far enough to give good clearance. After you have passed

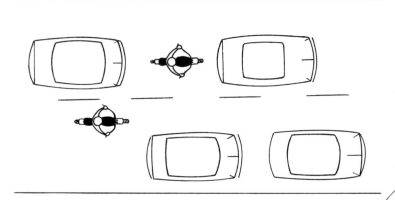

Note how the cyclist in the right lane has greater visibility ahead than the rider in the left lane, who has positioned himself directly back of the car in front. Do not, however, ride on the line, but keep far enough inside that you will not be side-swiped by cars in the opposite lane.

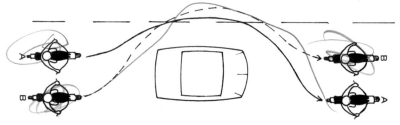

When riding in pairs, cycle A passes first, after making sure that the right of way is clear; cycle A then moves to the right side of the road in front of the car, leaving room for cycle B to follow and take his place on the left side.

far enough to see the car you passed in your rear-view mirror, lean to the right and swing back into your original lane.

The Wrong Way to Pass

There are times when a rider is tempted to forget the rules and pass to the right of the car ahead. One is when traffic is heavy and an inviting asphalted shoulder stretches out in front of him. For miles ahead traffic is bumper-to-bumper, but the paved shoulder is completely empty. In five minutes you could cover as many miles on the shoulder as you could in an hour in the traffic jam.

Yet to turn off is not only illegal but dangerous. The shoulders on our highways were put there partly to protect the main roadway from erosion and partly to provide a safety zone onto which cars can pull when in trouble.

When you use the shoulders to take shortcuts around jammed traffic, you have no way of knowing when a car in front of you will need to pull out of the traffic lane. He will not be expecting you to come zipping along and you will not be expecting him to turn out. Two such surprises can add up to one messy collision.

These shoulders are also broken by incoming ramps that will lead you right into the face of oncoming traffic. In places the shoulders narrow down and in others they are cut by drainage ditches that are sheer disaster for a cyclist. The shoulders should be used for what they were intended to be: an emergency stopping zone.

When Right Is Wrong Again

In the last section we were talking about passing on the right side of a car on a freeway or highway. It is equally suicidal to try to pass on the right-hand side of a car in city streets.

An experience of a cycling friend of mine clearly shows

the danger. The rider was intending to corner at the next intersection. There was a gap between the car ahead and the right-hand curb. My friend headed through it, but as he drew alongside the car he did not see that the driver had flicked on his turn signals. The car also intended to turn at the same intersection.

Luckily the motorcycle rider realized what was happened. He jumped the curb, narrowly missing being knocked down by the turning car. It was a close shave and one that taught him why one should never try to pass between a car and the curb.

The possibility of being cut off by a turning car is but one of the hazards of right-hand passing. Quite a few riders over the years have found themselves slammed up against suddenly opening doors of parked cars, or braking like mad to avoid a pedestrian who thoughtlessly stepped off the curb, or swerving frantically to avoid a child. Still another hazard is the possibility of slamming into a car pulling out from the curb or from a driveway.

Parking

Every ride must end sometime. Ordinarily a beginner does not foresee problems in parking. After all, a motorcycle is small and a rider does not have the difficulties that a beginner in an automobile has when it comes to shoving big cars into small spaces.

Yet parking motorcycles sometimes give rise to problems. If, like California, your state requires you to park your cycle with one wheel always touching the curb, you can have some trouble if your bike is equipped with a rear wheelstand.

If you have a jiffy or kickstand on the side, you simple wheel into position with the front or back wheel touching the curb, knock down the stand, and lean the bike. That's all there is to it.

But with the rear wheelstand, you drop the stand and then push the cycle back so that the stand goes under the back wheel, lifting it off the pavement. Beginners find it difficult to judge just how far the machine will move backward when they push it up on the stand. Thus they invariably fail to touch the curb or else are so close to the curb that they can't roll back far enough to get the stand in place.

Incidently, starting from a parked position is even more critical than going into a parking spot. In the first case about the worst a beginner can do is bump the curb or fray his temper. But leaving a parking place can be extremely dangerous.

It is obvious that you should look around and make sure that you aren't moving out into a collision course with flowing traffic. Not so obvious is the need for sufficient clear room to maneuver even if the street or parking area is clear of other moving traffic.

This is a very important point and one that has piled up more than a few beginners. Motorcycles, because of their smaller size, can be parked almost anywhere. As a result there is often little clear space around them. You may turn out and face a wall a few feet away. Or it may be a parked car, a tree, a house, a hedge, or another obstruction.

Unfamiliar with the capabilities of their machines, many beginners overestimate their ability to guide and control their cycles. They plow right into the obstructions.

When operating in close quarters, it is better to push your machine to a sufficiently clear area before mounting until you learn exactly what you can do within a certain area.

Of course, never attempt to push your bike in traffic.

Chapter 6

SPECIAL PROBLEMS OF STREET AND ROAD

In reviewing statistics on accidents involving all kinds of motor vehicles, it appears that intersections are the most fertile ground for trouble.

Possibly the most common cause of this trouble is the yellow traffic light. All too many drivers speed up when they should be slowing down because they are eager to "make the light" and avoid stopping for the coming red light.

The law concerning traffic lights is generally that the purpose of the yellow light is to clear the intersection of moving traffic so that cross-traffic can moving with the coming green light. The important point here is the word "clear." You are not helping to clear the intersection if you attempt to charge across on the yellow light.

Many drivers think they are on the right side of the law if they can just get into the intersection before the light turns red. Generally, under most local traffic codes, this is not true. You can enter the intersection on a yellow light. You may be so close that stopping suddenly would cause a pileup behind you. However, if you enter the cross-traffic section so late on the yellow that the red light catches you still trying to cross, then you are guilty of an unsafe practice and eligible for a traffic ticket.

More and more states are beginning to keep figures on moving-traffic violators. Points are assessed for each violation and your driving record will be checked both by highway departments and insurance companies. Too many points and your insurance—already so high that it often costs more than your vehicle—jumps up. Also, too many points may have you walking again after the highway department revokes your driving license.

So you can see there is a practical and financial reason for watching those yellow lights in addition to the safety angle of keeping you alive.

From the standpoint of the motorcyclists, intersections have several special dangers. All the trouble does not come with trying to make the yellow. Jumping the green —that is, trying to get off to an extra-fast start—can also be disastrous.

When you dart off too soon, having glimpsed the flash of yellow in the other lane and expecting the green, you may find yourself arguing for space with a car that is trying to run the yellow in the cross-lane. When your 150-, 350- or 650-pound mount tangles with a 2,200-pound car, the car is going to win every time.

You are also handicapped because a driving fool trying to make another light and save himself ten seconds usually has his eyes on the light and he isn't paying attention to you as you're trying to jump the green. When you ride a cycle you are doubly handicapped because your smaller size make it more difficult for speeding drivers to see you coming in at an angle.

Tunnel Vision

You'll also find this tunnel vision, as it is called, working against you when you are approaching a car that intends to make a left turn in front of you. In such cases you definitely have the right of way. No driver has any right to turn in front of you. Having the right of way may be a good argument for your heirs' lawyers, but it will not get you a reduced price at the undertaker's.

Turning out in front of cycles is a very common danger. Many times it happens that the car driver just doesn't see the oncoming cycle. He is limited by his tunnel vision. There are also times when he does see the cycle and feels he can bluff the rider of the smaller vehicle into slowing down.

Or, to give him credit for not being completely a bully, maybe he honestly thinks he can make the turn before the cycle plows into him. Many drivers will take chances with a cycle approaching that they would never take if the oncoming vehicle were another car or a truck.

Since you are the little guy, it is up to you to be always on the defensive. You must think ahead, drive ahead, and generally be smarter than the road hogs. The best rule for intersections is to go slow, looking for vehicles that may cut into your lane from left or right and keeping an eye out for any cars in the left turn lane.

The Guy Who Walks

All the hazards of street and road aren't caused by drivers. The guy who walks contributes his share as well. At any moment someone may step out from between two parked cars, walking around to get in his own. Or he may suddenly open a door to get out, presenting himself and his opened door directly in the path of your oncoming cycle.

These are very possible dangers. However, insurance figures show that more pedestrians get hurt at intersections than at any other place. This presents another danger to watch out for.

There are two major danger points where motorcycles, pedestrians, and intersections are involved. One is when you make a right turn just as a pedestrian decides to make his mad dash across the street before the green walk sign goes red.

The other danger point is when the car in the lane next to you stops for a pedestrian and you can't see the person because the stopped car blocks your view.

The law requires traffic to stop when one car stops for a pedestrian. And of course, pedestrians in a cross-walk or intersection have the right of way. However, at an intersection where there are neither street lights or stop signs, it is not always possible to determine if the car on the curb side of you has stopped for a pedestrian or has halted in order to make a right turn.

This is true even if the stopped car is flashing his turn signals. There is a possibility that a pedestrian is crossing in front of him. The only safe thing to do is never to pass a stopped car until you are sure that he has not stopped for a reason that requires you to stop also.

Braking in the Turn

There is one last word we should add before leaving the hazards of intersections. This is about making your own turn. It is self-evident that you should watch oncoming traffic and proceed only when it is safe. For some reason many riders follow these precautions, which they learned driving cars, and then ignore one of the surest ways to disaster on a cycle: improper braking on curves and when cornering.

When you approach an intersection to turn, the time to apply the brakes is well in advance of the point where you actually start cornering. Unless you are facing an absolute emergency, it is never wise to apply brakes when you are actually turning. You are asking for a skid and a spill if you do.

How far ahead of the corner you brake depends of course upon your speed. After a little experience in turning, you know what is a safe speed to make your turn. Brake far enough in advance of the corner, begin your turn, and pick up speed as you curve around.

If an emergency demands that you apply the brake in a corner, use the rear brake until you are at an almost upright angle. Then slowly apply your front brake.

The Changing Road

It is equally important to brake cautiously if the corner or street is slippery. The condition of a street or road changes constantly. This is a severe handicap to cyclists. Loose dirt, gravel, a smear of grease, dripped oil, or even a patch of ice that has not thawed are all common hazards that can throw a cycle out of control. Items that would be dismissed entirely by autoists loom as tremendous obstacles to the motorcyclist.

If some of these hazards seem trivial, consider this experience reported by one cyclist: "It had been raining and I stopped to have a cup of coffee until it let up. After that, I cut my speed until the sun dried the highway. I thought, 'Man, the safety director would be proud to see me now!' And he should have been. I was going right by the rules he'd taught us. Then as the road dried I picked up speed to make up for the time I'd lost sitting out the rain.

"Mind you, I wasn't traveling at an excessive speed. I was playing it by the book. Then I came to a sharp curve. I slowed just like I'm supposed to and went into the curve at a safe speed. Then as I started to come out of the curve I saw that the wind had blown a lot of leaves up on the roadbed.

"Okay, leaves. They don't make much of a bump, I figured, but when I hit them my front wheel went thisaway, my back wheel went thataway. By some miracle I stayed upright until the skid took my mount off the shoulder and into hedges along the roadbed. I wasn't hurt, but I learned then that wet leaves are as slippery as a greased pig."

Litter Trouble

The lesson to be learned from this cyclist's fall is that you must question every new situation. Road conditions can be expected to change all the time. That is the only general thing you can depend upon. One cyclist took a spin because he wasn't following the good-cyclist advice to ride to the side so he could see up the line of cars. He considered this risky, so he kept directly behind the car in front.

"I keep far enough back so there is no danger of my tail-ending the car in front," he stubbornly insisted. "I can stop easily enough in an emergency."

And he could. But he forgot that preventing a rear-end crash was only one of the reasons why a motorcyclist should ride where he can see down the traffic line. One day he learned one of the other reasons.

This time the traffic flow stopped suddenly. He braked without difficulty, although the car back of him barely missed ramming into the cycle's rear end. However, we'll admit that this wasn't the cyclist's fault. So far so good. Then when the traffic began to move our friend suddenly felt that sinking feeling riders get when they no longer have control. Fortunately he wasn't moving fast and the car behind had time to stop before it ran over him as he took a hard spill.

What happened was that the car ahead had an oil leak. Dripping faster with the car stopped, it left a small puddle, and the motorcycle's front wheel slipped in it.

This story again shows that the only thing you can really depend upon is the unexpected. Such stories about freak accidents are not intended to dampen your spirit as a beginner. Motorcycling has plenty to make it worthwhile. However, these things do happen, and almost invariably they are the result of the rider's not following the rules. Our friend who skidded on the leaves should have known that wet leaves are slippery. Likewise, if the other rider had been riding off-center, as instructors advise, he would not have skidded in the oil puddle.

Probably you'll meet more trouble from just plain litter than you will from occasional oil spills and wet leaves. A broken bottle, glass from a previous automobile accident, pieces of wire, boxes, and even scattered vegetables have been reported with these and other road litter.

Just Keep Your Eyes on the Road

It doesn't take much imagination to understand what a broken bottle can do to a tire, but many beginners don't realize the danger of other types of litter. If you see a large object on the road, you naturally go around it, but you may not be so careful with something like a piece of wire. Yet the wire can be more dangerous than something big. All it has to do is get caught in your wheel or sprocket and you have suddenly added a home-made brake. Such a brake applied suddenly at the wrong time and in an un-controlled manner can send the cycle in one direction and you in another.

Litter that lies in the road is bad enough, but debris that moves is still worse. A case in point was the fix a rider found himself in when a muffler fell off a jalopy in front of him. The muffler with a piece of tailpipe hit the pave-ment, bounced, and changed directions twice as it kept bouncing.

The rider saw it fall and leaned to the right to curve around the piece of wreckage. Then he found himself and it on a collision course as the muffler ricocheted again. He managed to dodge his way out of the tight corner, but, as he later explained, that was when he got his first clump of gray hairs.

Again, you can avoid such hazards only by keeping your eyes on the road and being alert every second. This is why you were taught from the beginning to learn the operation of your controls so well that you could handle them unconsciously. Then you can give your undivided attention to the road and its many hazards.

Night Riding

High up on our list of special hazards is night riding. A basic rule for all vehicle drivers is to slow down at sundown. Your vision as a driver is greatly decreased at night, making normal road hazards harder to see. And possibly of greater importance, your cycle will be even more difficult to see in the dark than an automobile.

There have been reports of accidents where cars tail-ended motorcycles because the driver, seeing the small taillight, thought the cycle was farther in front of him than it really was.

A light-colored cycle is good insurance here. Also a white helmet and a light-colored jacket help you to be seen at night. Dark cycles and dark leather jackets only add to your chances of getting hit.

Another important night-riding point is to keep your windshield clean if you have one. The same is true of your goggles and your face shield, if your helmet has one to replace your goggles. Dirty goggles or shields scatter incoming light, causing blurs in your vision and making details indistinct.

The main thing to remember here is that all the normal road hazards that confront you during the day are doubled, trebled, and possibly quadrupled at night. This is no reason for parking your mount and starting to walk when the sun sets, but it does call for adding an extra measure of caution. Remember the old, old advice they give drivers: "Drive as if everybody else on the road were an idiot and you'll be okay."

This, of course, is an exaggeration. *All* drivers on the road are not idiots—just the majority of them!

Riding in the Rain

If night riding compounds a rider's hazards, riding in the rain compounds the compounds. Here you are not only faced with the problem of decreased visibility but find new handicaps, like loss of traction plus extra debris often washed on the roadbed by high water.

In fair weather the sun and the wind are pleasant, but when the rain starts falling, lack of a roof over your head becomes a distinct liability. Goggles and faceshields, a necessity for protecting a rider's eyes from airborne dust and insects, become an impossible handicap in the rain. There are no windshield wipers on goggles and helmet faceshields. The raindrops that "keep falling on your head" will blur and distort your vision until it will be impossible for you to see the road and traffic.

Taking your goggles off is not much help, either. The rain slamming into your bare face is also blinding. This is true even of a light rain. The speed with which raindrops slam into your face is compounded by your own speed. The faster you go the harder the rain-slam against you. While you need to slow your speed in the rain, you can't drop to a crawl or some car will be rear-ending you.

Other Hazards

Lowered visibility is not the only rainy-day hazard for motorcyclists. You will get soaking-wet regardless of how well you are dressed. Wet boots may slip on the gear or brake just when you need them. Wet gloves may also slip on the gas throttle. You could find yourself in a tight spot with your controls failing to respond properly just when you need them the most.

And while tires are treaded to squeegee the road and dry it off for proper traction on wet pavement, they can't take care of a lot of natural slipperyness. Large puddles of water on the highway are another problem. Hit one of those and at best a sheet of blinding water splashes over you. At worst you may either slip or drown out your engine.

There is actually no "best" way to drive in the rain. The smart rider either stays at home on rainy days or, if caught in a sudden downpour, stops somewhere until it lets up.

PART 2:

CYCLE FUN

Chapter 7

THE CALL OF THE OPEN ROAD

After listening to so much "do this" and "don't do that," the beginner can well start to wonder when the fun of cycling starts.

The answer is that the fun commences when you solo for the first time, and grows with each succeeding ride. All the do's and the don'ts are merely rules developed from the sad experience of others to keep the fun in your motorcycling. These rules are important, but after a while many of them become automatic in your mind. You won't have to give them a thought. You'll just follow them at the proper time.

If the back of your neck itches, you don't have to think that you should scratch, ponder over which hand to use and which fingernail. You just scratch without consciously worrying about the details. It will get to be the same with many of your motorcycle operations.

One thing that should never become automatic, however, is keeping alert for road hazards. But once you note them, after you have gained a lot of experience riding, it will not be necessary to worry about what to do. When your eyes spot the danger, your reflexes take over.

Road Riding

Motorcycle racing gets the most publicity, but there is another side of cycling. With 1971 registrations estimated at 2.8 million, there are probably two million bike riders

This couple is well equipped for road riding. They have a windshield for partial protection, helmets, and windbreakers, and their baggage is securely fastened to the rear behind the passenger. The machine appears to be a 350-cc Honda.

who have never competed in organized races. Yet they get just as much frun from their machines as any of the competition boys.

These noncompetition sportsters call themselves "Road Riders." To them a motorcycle is an enjoyable mount to get on and get out and just run. The kick comes from just "riding along with the wind" and stopping here and there to study the wonders of nature. Since Road Riders are generally a friendly, gregarious lot, they band together in clubs, ride together in groups, and end up their day's run with cycle games.

Passengers should never be carried except on a pillion seat behind the rider. The passenger must keep his or her feet on the special passenger pegs to keep from disturbing the balance or hitting obstacles. The driver here is Michael Parks, star of the former TV show "Then Came Bronson." (NBC-TV Photo.)

In this type of fun riding you will find every type of person and every possible age. The American Motorcycle Association reports having road members who have been straddling a motor bike for fifty years. At the other end of the scale are riders just barely old enough to qualify for their drivers' licenses. This age varies in different states.

Drivers' licenses are required for all riding on public streets and highways. On private land where no license

There is no age limit for off-road motorcycling where drivers' and vehicle licenses are not required. Here a twelve-year-old heads his bike toward a sandy stretch of desert.

is required, the only age restriction is just to be big enough for your legs to touch the ground when you straddle whatever size bike you can ride.

Club Runs

Generally when a bike rider speaks of "competition" he means all-out racing. However, clubs have their own competitions which do not have anything to do with racing of the formal track type.

Club runs can take almost any form. In its most elemental form a club run can be no more than a group of congenial people taking off together for an afternoon of touring the highways and back roads. Generally, however, the planners put in some competition along the way and then end the run with a field meet where you may find yourself teamed against your running mates in a wide variety of games.

One of the most popular road-run competitions is the "Poker Run." While details may vary according to the program chairman planning the event, here is the way it is generally done:

The course is plotted for anywhere from a hundred to two hundred miles, with 150 to 175 being the average. At the start all participants are given a route map, which shows you the way to go, checkpoints along the way, and, if possible, where directional signs are located.

At the five checkpoints along the way, you will pick up one ordinary playing card at each point. At the conclusion of the run you will then have five cards, which make up a draw poker-playing hand. The winner is the rider with the best hand.

In some cases the checkpoint attendant has a box of

folded and stapled cards. Riders check in and take a card from the box. In remote areas where there is sufficient room to park and roam, the cards may be scattered around and you have to dismount and hunt for one.

Other clubs may find the card per checkpoint too much trouble. These merely give riders a poker chip or piece of paper showing that they checked in at each point. Then at the conclusion of the run, all those with five chips are entitled to be dealt a hand of poker. The winning hand is declared the rider of the day as in the other method.

Field Days

Club runs often end with overnight stops and fun field events. At the latter you will find all manner of games played on and with motorcycles. Such field events are pretty much like the games you've played at school, company, or Fourth of July picnics—with the important difference that you play them from the seat of a cycle.

These games take many forms. A popular one is the stake race. Stakes are driven in the ground to make a narrow runway. The object is to weave your way through them, passing the first stake on the right, the second on the left, the third back on the right side and so on. Variations include substituting barrels or bales of hay or similar objects for the stakes.

Play Ball!

Ball games are also played from the backs of motorcycles. Kickball is a popular one. Two teams line up on their cycles facing each other. The leadoff man kicks the ball toward the opposing team's goal line. Then the scramble is on, each side trying to kick, butt, or slap the ball and score for his side. A game like this, although the cycles never get up sufficient speed to really hurt anyone, can get rough. For this reason it is well to dress in the heavy protective leather clothing that racing riders use. You won't have to use as much liniment the next day.

While they are not as popular as kickball, there have been field meets featuring such unlikely motorcycle sports as cycle hockey, cycle polo, and cycle baseball.

A cycle baseball game is quite a riot to watch and a headache to play. Every player except the catcher is required to play from the saddle of his machine, as a general rule. However, one group I once knew permitted the batter to dispense with the cycle after a fast ball knocked out a headlight. As soon as he made a hit, the batter had to climb on his cycle for the run to the bases.

Other Games

Another popular game is the "Slow Race." Here the object is to be the *last* to cross the finish line. The difficulty comes from the fact that you aren't permitted to stop. And you are disqualified if you have to put your foot on the ground to keep from falling over.

You'll also see the "teeter-totter" at just about every field meet. Here a board is laid over a block. The object may be to ride over it like a seesaw. Again the object may be to ride just as far up the board as possible without causing it to tilt down on the other side, then back off again. Still another variation is to ride up the incline on one side of the fulcrum, balance in the center, and rocking back and forth from this point to make an up-and-down seesaw.

Also popular as a cycle game is barrel rolling. In this game contestants put their front tires against barrels which are turned on their sides. The object is to push the barrel over the finish line before your opponents. If any part of the cycle touches the barrel except with the front tire, the rider is disqualified.

This is called "cutting hay." The monkey (passenger) on a side car motorcycle racer leans out so far on a turn that he hits weeds growing along the side of the asphalt track.

One of the biggest thrillers in professional motorcycle racing is the side car race, also called hacks. Low-slung, speedy bikes, they sometimes reach speeds of 120 mph. The passenger, called a monkey in the slang of the track, has to take many strange and dangerous positions to keep the hack balanced as it streaks around corners. Here one leans over so far that there is scarcely an inch between the seat of his leather pants and the asphalt race track.

The idea of picking up objects while moving on the cycle is the basis of several games. One of the more popular is to place balls or similar objects on top of soft-drink bottles arranged at intervals down the course. The rider has to pick the balls off without upsetting the bottle or stopping. A variation is to have the riders try to

Starting young are these pre-teen mini-cycle fans who are practicing on the mini-bike track at Indian Dunes, California. Such tracks as these are teaching youngsters the principles of motorcycle safety. Note the "hot shot" turning technique of the youngster on the right.

put balls on top of bottles. Still another variation is to make riders move at a predetermined speed and try to throw balls into baskets along the route.

Road Machines

At field meets you will find just about every kind of cycle made. Minibikes are popular and the lighter trail bikes are good for close-in games where fast maneuvering is needed. Heavy road "hogs" are at a disadvantage

Heavy machines, like this Harley-Davidson in the foreground, and the Moto-Guzzi just behind it, are made for touring and long road running where power is needed. Note the heavily padded seat for comfort on long drives, the shift lever which can be worked with both toe and heel, and the footboard that takes the place of the usual foot peg. This is a 750-cc engine.

here because they can't turn as fast as the smaller machines.

For long-distance runs and touring the bigger machines are what you need. Their power comes in handy climbing mountains, passing on the highway, and in keeping up with the traffic flow. Also, their greater horsepower permits loading on more equipment and camping gear.

Front tires on motorcycles have treads that wrap around the sidewalls to hold traction when cornering. It is important that tires worn slick or becomes "peaked" from much cornering.

You'll also find the bigger machines less tiring on long hauls. Fatigue is a problem that road runners have to contend with. Fatigue leads to inattention and inattention to trouble.

There are many varieties of cycles and each is designed for a specific job. You can double up and ride a road machine on mountain trails, but you'll wish you had a lighter bike before you get home. Similarly, you can tour on a light bike (if it has sufficient horsepower to qualify for freeway riding), but we don't recommend it.

Many special-purpose bikes are not ridden on roads and streets. They are carried in pickups, on the backs of campers, and on racks attached to car bumpers. Such bikes do not have to be registered (as of now) and you don't need a drivers' license if you keep off public thoroughfares.

Many cycles like this Montesa are never ridden on public streets and highways. They are carried to private tracks. Such machines do not require registration.

The American Motorcycle Association

A beginner wanting to join in the fun of cycling quickly can do nothing better than to join a cycle club. There are hundreds of them devoted to all phases of the sport. Regardless of whether your interest is road running, drag racing, motocross, off-road racing, flat track racing, or just family fun, you'll find a club composed of enthusiasts who will welcome you if you are willing to abide by the club's rules—and, of course, pay your dues.

In addition to individual clubs, there are also a number of associations devoted to bringing the clubs together, formulating rules, plugging safety, and generally working for the betterment of motorcycling as a whole. To name just a few, there are the American Federation of Motorcyclists, Baja Racing Association, Classic and Antique Motorcycle Association, National Off Road Racing Association, and many others.

The most famous of them all and the one that has worked hardest to improve motorcycling's image is the American Motorcycle Association, with headquarters in Columbus, Ohio. The AMA was organized in 1924 and has helped the sport for forty-eight years.

The association serves motorcycling in two ways. One is its vigorous public relations program to acquaint the general public with the true picture of the sport, counteracting the "Wild Bunch" and "Easy Rider" image hung on motorcycling by newspaper scare stories and lurid movies.

The second way AMA serves the sport is in formulating competition rules and sanctioning meets and races. In the first half-century that the association has been fighting for the improvement of cycling, it increased the safety of cycling, built up organized cycle racing, and succeeded in getting racing purses increased. AMA has also worked closely with manufacturers to improve the quality of cycles and cycle equipment. And its technical staff has worked out the most stringent rules that member clubs must enforce to insure safe riding in AMA-sanctioned competitions.

AMA and Its Critics

While just about everyone admits that AMA has done a great job for cycling, the organization has its critics. These are notably among road riders who feel that AMA is more interested in competition and competition riders and does not pay sufficient attention to the problems of those who ride just for the fun of it.

This feeling has led to the formation of other organizations devoted to aiding clubs restricted to specific motorcycling activity. One of the fastest-growing associations of this kind is the Southern California Motorcycle Association (SCMA). This association is strictly for road riders, according to its president, Doug Berger, and will never be anything else but a road riders' group.

"The main thing we are doing," he says, "is giving the road rider an association of, by, and for road riders."

Although its name, Southern California Motorcycle Association, would appear to restrict SCMA to a region, its officers report that such is not the case. It has member clubs all the way to the east coast and is developing into a national organization.

SCMA is extremely concerned with improving the image of motorcycle riders. Before any club can become affiliated with the organization the applicant is carefully investigated.

"The SCMA is constantly striving to improve the Road Riders' image by establishing a rapport with law-enforcement bodies and leaders of our communities. This is slowly enabling the general public to see past the barrier that was set up by groups such as Hell's Angels. When people do see beyond this barrier, they find that just because a person rides a motorcycle it does not mean that he is any different than when he drives an auto," Berger says.

Famous Road Runs

The thrill of violent action and intense competition that one gets in racing and various scrambles is missing in road riding, but the people who prefer road riding to competition are a different class from the gung-ho competitors. Some of their group road runs have become classics. The most famous was the truly mammoth Death Valley Run that began in 1954.

This run was held in October with riders from all over the western states converging on Death Valley in California in what was described as the "World Series" of motorcycle road riding. The promoters' idea was to give road riding something that would gain public attention. Death Valley was picked as the site because of its historic importance in the history of the West and the gold rush days, because of its magnificent scenery, and because it had all the space necessary to ride and ride and ride.

The original 1954 run drew 200 riders. Within five years it was drawing 2,500 cyclists. It was eventually stopped because it grew too big.

There are still a large number of long road runs around. It is difficult to list them because they change often. As suburbs expand, areas where large groups of cyclists can congregate grow less with the years.

The great popularity of road riding is shown by the large crowds who attend even the small 75- to 150-mile rides. For its first run of 1971, the Majestic Motorcyclists, a Whittier-based California group, sent out invitations.

They got 829 riders who came from as far as 530 miles away to ride with the group.

Another club in northern California set up to accommodate 200 riders for its first run that same season but drew 348 without even plugging the event.

All this seems to point up the fact—as road-rider associations have been trying to tell us for a long time—that there are far more cyclists in the road-rider category than there are all-out competition riders, and they are just as enthusiastic.

Road Riding in Safety

We have covered most of the general hazards of the road that road riders will probably encounter. There are a few however, that should be mentioned which were not covered earlier. One of these hazards is large trucks.

Truckdrivers are by and large a fine body of people. Drivers, trucking companies, and the various unions have gone out of their way to create a public image of truckdrivers as gentlemen of the road. And it is true that the boys who chauffeur the big rigs will give other drivers a fair deal—which is more than most automobile drivers will give other drivers.

However, we can't deny the fact that a big rig (as truckers call their combinations) is a giant of the road and that a motorcycle is a pygmy beside it. This calls for a few precautions on the part of the cyclist.

Even in an automobile with its far greater weight, you can feel the suction shake a car when a big truck passes you. This is specially true when you are riding in a strong side wind. When the truck passes you or you pass it, a lot of this side wind is suddenly blocked by the solid bulk of the huge trailers. As a motorcycle rider you have been

—perhaps unconsciously—leaning into the wind to compensate for its force as you zipped along. The sudden blocking of this wind by the truck can cause you to swerve dangerously. It could even pile you into the side of the truck if conditions are right.

There is no particular danger if you realize that the hazard exists and shift your body as motorcycle and truck pass.

Let Him Know You're There

You must always remember that your small size makes you hard to see. If you pull in close behind a big truck in heavy highway traffic and then, when you see an opening, suddenly whip around him, you are begging for trouble. Polite as he is supposed to be, he is only human. He has the same reaction-delay lag as the rest of us. You must give him time to react.

Similarly, be careful about stopping in front of trucks and cutting in front of them at intersections. These big rigs can't stop as fast as automobiles. Don't try to argue with a truck over who has the right of way. It is poor consolation to win an argument if you lose your life.

About Your Passenger

On these road runs you'll often see riders carrying passengers. Sometimes it's a rider with a buddy or a girl friend. At other times, since road-riding is often a family affair, you may see ma and pa astride their own machines with the kids propped up in back.

Carrying passengers is legal enough and safe if done correctly. Generally the law provides that you can carry a passenger only on a seat to the rear of the driver. This seat must be securely fastened to the machine. Separate foot pegs and a hand grip must always be provided for the passenger.

These rules are based on sound safety principles. If the passenger's legs are permitted to dangle instead of resting on the foot pegs, there is danger of a foot striking some obstacle in the road or even getting entangled in the rear-wheel spokes. Also, these dangling legs are likely to upset the driver's control of his machine.

All authorities agree that it is unwise for a beginner to carry a passenger. The balance is quite different. As you know, turns, except at very low speeds, are made by leaning in the direction you wish to turn. If a passenger is on the rear seat, hanging on to the driver, his leaning also affects the cycle's control. An experienced cyclist can make adjustments for this which a novice cannot do.

All this applies to passengers on rear seats (pillion or "pad"). Passengers in sidecars are even more of a problem. Cycles equipped with sidecars—or any customized three-wheel cycle—cannot be steered by leaning as we do our two-wheelers. They must be steered like a car. There is also the problem of centrifugal force lifting the sidecar off the pavement on turns.

Riding in Pairs

On road runs riders frequently pair off or ride in groups. It is well then to know how to pass cars while riding in pairs. Ordinarily two cycles abreast are enough in one lane, and the procedure for passing while riding in pairs is merely expanded to take care of the whole group.

When two cyclists approach a car to pass we will consider the cycle on the left as cycle A and the one on the right as cycle B. (Note accompanying diagram.)

When it comes time to pass, cycle A checks oncoming traffic in the adjacent lane, and by checking rear-view mirror and taking a quick backward glance, insures that no traffic behind him is also pulling out to pass.

Once he is assured that there are no traffic hazards, he pulls out and around the car in front. When he is far enough ahead of the car he is passing, cycle A cuts back into his original lane, *moving over to the right side of the road in the position formerly occupied by cycle B,* but in front of the car.

As soon as cycle A pulls out to make his pass, cycle B moves over into the left position formerly occupied by cycle A. This is done so that B can easily look down the line of traffic and ascertain for himself if the way is clear for him to pass.

Under no circumstances should cycle B depend upon cycle A's determination of safety and blindly follow the first cycle. He should make his own determination. Traffic conditions can change rapidly. A hole big enough for cycle A to pass safely may close before B can move out.

After cycle B determines that it is safe to pass, he curves around the car in front and then curves back into the original lane paralleling his companion, taking his position on the left side of cycle A.

In this manner the two cyclists have swapped positions in the maneuver. This is done to give cycle B a spot to move into without having to fall back between the car they are passing and cycle A in front of it.

If there is a group of cyclists running together, they can make their pass in a similar manner.

Chapter 8

COUNTRY ROADS AND TRAILS

Country roads have their own problems. A country road may be defined as any road that goes through the country, but for our purpose we will skip freeways and turnpikes. We'll talk of the smaller roads that branch out through rural sections of the country.

Many of these roads were not planned. They just grew or happened. They are often narrow with very little shoulder and confined to two lanes of traffic—one in each direction. Passing puts you directly in the face of oncoming traffic.

Worse yet, many of these roads are cut by a multitude of crossroads that offer the worst in visibility. Trees, shrubs, and even weeds keep you from seeing who and what is approaching on the other road. Turns are almost right angles without banking which means that a prudent driver will slow to a crawl to corner.

You will also find poor upkeep on many of these roads. Broken pavement, cracks, and gravel and debris add to the hazards for the motorcyclist. Flat land is bad enough, but if the road stretches into hilly country, you'll find

102

yourself fighting hairpin turns. Fallen rocks are another hazard to watch for. In areas where the roadbed has been scraped through hills to reduce grades, rocks on the highway can be sufficiently large to upset a speeding cycle.

In these mountainous sections you can also zip over a grade too fast and find yourself tailgating a slow car that has been hidden back of the summit. You may even find one stalled from overheating or other causes. If you are facing heavy oncoming traffic on these narrow roads, you will not be able to go around him. Road conditions don't always permit you to come to a fast braking stop. You can start to skid very easily on some of these roads. Broadsliding on a narrow mountain road may throw you directly into opposing traffic on one side or over the edge of a bluff on the other. The choice is not good, I'm afraid, either way.

Dips, Ice, and Water

Dips have been so well engineered on highways that they are not a problem, but on these rural roads you'll still find them. Faced with the problem of water, instead of going to the expense of putting in a culvert, the road builders just put in a dip for the water to run over. Such dips are usually of concrete in an otherwise asphalt road. They can bounce a cycle and turn the hapless rider into an unwilling gymnast.

Sometimes you'll find these dips full of water, and not always only after a rain when you might be expecting them. Irrigation runoffs from farms can also fill them up on occasion. The trouble is that not only is the crossing slippery but any number of other hazards may have been washed up on the pavement by the water. Often it is so dirty that you can't see what is underneath.

A rider who blindly splashes through at top speed may go on while his cycle lies down and gives up. In case you have never kept traveling after your cycle stopped, let me assure you that it is a most unpleasant feeling.

Another danger of these mountain roads is the possibility of hitting ice even though it may be well into spring or early summer. A section of the road shaded by a steep slope may not have received enough sun to thaw out completely.

Just Take It Easy

Here again, all of these road hazards are being successfully skirted by thousands of riders every weekend. The secret, as it is in all kinds of motorcycle riding, is to take things easy when you need to take it easy. You don't have to crawl along the road, fearful of every bump. But you do have to take care not to override your vision. It is pretty much like night driving: never go so fast that you overrun your headlights so that you can't stop if an obstacle suddenly pops up. On these country roads you don't open up to the maximum speed limit unless you can see far enough down the road to know what you are riding into.

This also means being alert to highway signs and paying attention to what they say. One you'll find in many mountain or park locations reads "Animal Crossing." You can find yourself arguing the right of way with a deer, a horse, or even (in places like Yellowstone National Park) a bear.

The animals you meet on the highway don't have to be big ones like deer or strayed cattle and sheep to cause you trouble. There is a documented case of a rider who had a jackrabbit run head-on into his front wheel on a West Texas road. Those Texas jackrabbits are tough. And while the front wheel made mincemeat of the poor desert bunny, the collision cost the rider a new front wheel, a replacement job on his handlebars, and several weeks' time regrowing a large patch of hide he wore off as he slid through the sand and cactus.

A Doggone Tough Time

Jackrabbits are not going to get entangled in everybody's spokes. Neither will every rider meet a cow in the road or argue with a Yellowstone bear. But dogs are something that most riders tangle with sooner or later.

Dogs are man's best friend only if the man is not a motorcycle rider. In big cities where leash laws are in effect to prevent dogs from running loose there is no problem. In other places you may be faced with an angry dog diving at your front wheel at any time.

A barking dog is more than just an annoyance. He is a potential danger. He can get wrapped up in your front wheel, grab your leg, and generally mess things up. The actor Keenan Wynn spent months in a hospital, barely pulling through, after a barking dog attracted his attention during a ride. He looked down and failed to see a car making a right turn directly in front of him.

Just how to cope with motorcycle-chasing dogs is something motorcyclists haven't entirely agreed on. Some suggest slowing down and then speeding up suddenly to leave Rover behind. Trying to outrun a dog is practical only in areas where you can get sufficient speed. Some dogs can run faster than others. I once had to hit

Trail riders can expect trouble and should be prepared with tire-repair materials and a small tool kit.

Cyclists must be prepared for any emergency. Here a young trail bike rider kicks up the sand in a fast stop when he sees a fallen log and another cyclist on a collision course with him.

25 miles per hour to draw away from a collie. Dogs with short legs, of course, can't do as well.

Off the Road

The hazards and troubles you'll encounter on the back roads are nothing compared to the obstacles that get in your way when you go off the road. Yet despite this, one of the fastest growing fields in motorcycling is off-the-road trail riding.

Trail riding appeals to those who like the wild outdoors. Many of the more enthusiastic trail riders today were not originally motorcyclists. They are sportsmen and out-doorsmen who discovered that the motorcycle, while it couldn't do everything that a mule could, was an excellent substitute for the old packhorse for hunting and fishing trips into wilderness areas.

While some die-hards take any kind of machine out on the trails, the best kind of cycle is a lightweight, stripped-down bike which has gained the name *trail bike*.

Keenan Wynn, who has been an enthusiastic rider for thirty years or more, tells in his autobiography why you need a special machine for trail riding.

On his first ride off the road, Wynn was surprised when his companions turned off the pavement and started up a narrow trail through some brush choking a rocky hill-side.

As Wynn tells it: " 'Where you going?' I hollered. Before anyone could answer I was flat on my back in the dust."

He goes on to relate how he fell several times before he realized that his big Harley just wasn't made to negoti-ate the twists and turns of a trail that was nothing more than a bulldozed firebreak that the Forestry Service had cut across the hills.

He wasn't the only Hollywood figure to learn the hard way that you need a lightweight, highly maneuverable machine stripped of anything that can catch and snag on

Actors Keenan Wynn, left, and Lee Marvin, Academy Award winning star, are both motorcycle fans. As you can see from their full leathers, helmets and goggles, both two-wheel veterans believe in observing safety rules. (NBC-TV Photo.)

the underbrush you must travel through. Wynn tells how the trail riders took Clark Gable out with them. Gable rode one of the biggest Triumphs money could buy. Gable was a pretty good cyclist, but had never tackled trail riding before. He just got moving up trail when his foot peg snagged on some obstruction. He was thrown, rolled down the rocky slope, and came to a jolting halt with his cycle on top of him.

His companions, who had learned the hard way themselves, gave the famous actor no sympathy. One yelled down to him, "Hey, Clark, what are you doing down there? The trail's up here!"

Trail Trimmed

You can generally spot a good trail bike. It is as spare as the old Model T was in its day. Fancy gadgets are for the road. The off-trail rider is smart to get rid of everything that is not absolutely essential. In addition to removing anything that might snag on brush, leaving the extras at home takes weight off the cycle and permits you to carry more camping gear, food, or an extra can of gasoline— not a bad idea at all.

The exhaust is usually pulled up high enough to clear streams that aren't too deep, and folding foot pegs are essential to driving in close quarters. Clearance between the engine and the ground should be greater than in a street bike, and a skid plate on the bottom and in front of the engine will keep the front wheel from throwing rocks back on the engine.

Under the right conditions and at the right speed it is possible for a cylinder to get cracked by a rock thrown up from the road. Also, there is a case on record of a trail rider who misjudged a stream. His engine was badly overheated from climbing when he plowed through a comparatively shallow stream. Perhaps he thought the spray would cool his engine. However, he hit an unexpectedly large rock in the water. He was knocked off balance and "laid it down" in the water. The cold mountain stream water hit the hot engine and the engine block cracked. He had a nice long walk home.

Cycles that will not be ridden on the public highways do not require such gear as headlights, turn signals, and such. For trail bike riding these can be dispensed with, unless you intend to drive at night. In that case you must have lights.

If lights are unnecessary, you might consider a bike with a magneto instead of a battery ignition. Earlier, in describing how two-stroke and four-stroke engines work, we mentioned that the spark plug provides the fire to ignite the gas mixture in the engine's cylinder.

In a battery ignition system, this electric spark originated in the battery. The current flows through the switch into a coil, where it is stepped up in intensity, and then into a distributor which sends the current to the spark plugs.

The magneto system works a little differently, although the final result is to get a high intensity spark to the terminals of the spark plug.

A flywheel magneto is actually a miniature dynamo in which a rotating armature connected to a circuit breaker is mounted between a permanent magnet. The rotation of the armature cutting the magnetic field produces an electric current. In a bike's magneto system, the magnet or magnets are built into the flywheel on the crankshaft. These together with a backplate carrying the coils, condenser, and contact breaker produce the six-volt electric current.

This generated current flows through the breaker points into a high-tension coil which increases the voltage so that the current is strong enough to jump the spark-plug gap.

Magnetos are most often found on minibikes, scooters, and lightweight motorcycles. They furnish sufficient current to fire the cylinder or cylinders, but if you need lights —and you must have them for public-thoroughfare use— you need a battery ignition system. The real advantage of the magneto system is that you get away from the weight and bulk of battery and generator.

Other things often seen on trail bikes are larger wheels, knobby tires that can bite into soft ground and hold traction, heavy-duty air cleaners to take care of the dust of off-road riding, large rear sprockets, and narrow handlebars so you can get through close places better.

We have already mentioned the higher clearance, the skid plate, and the higher-positioned exhaust. However, we should add also a need for a hydraulic dampening system in your front fork, vibration-proof bolts that won't jar loose on you, and a spark arrester on your exhaust. The spark arrester is essential in many areas, including national forests.

The Greatest Hazard

The greatest hazard to the rapidly growing off-the-road cycle fraternity is not nature but the cyclist's fellow man. More and more areas are being closed to cyclists. Cycle parks are under court attack to have them closed. Large sections of public lands where cyclists used to roam at will are now being declared off limits.

Part of this is the fault of cyclists themselves. They would roam an area without regard for ecology, wildlife, or those who must come after them. Cycling's enemies claimed off-the-roaders destroyed vegetation, scared game, littered wilderness areas with oil cans, blown-out tires, and rusting parts. Cycles were also charged with being a fire hazard and a noise polluter.

There is justification for these complaints, and the American Motorcycle Association and other cycling groups are working hard to improve cycling's image. Their work is of little good if cyclists themselves do not do their part. This means being courteous on the road and trail, observing tresspass rules and not crossing private property without permission, and yielding right of way to hikers and horseback riders.

It is also important to observe all posted signs when riding in national parks and forests. While mufflers have been required in towns all along, California recently led the way to force cyclists to keep mufflers on their vehicles in the back country as a means of lowering noise pollution. The new law requires mufflers "to prevent excessive or unusual noise" except in organized competition on closed courses.

Motorcycling's Friends

Many organized groups are fighting for the motorcycle. Homeowners and apartment owners are constantly getting petitions to close nearby cycle parks. Conservation groups are fighting the use of cycles on public land. Private owners are refusing cyclists permission to use their land. And municipalities are thinking up more restrictive laws and regulations. Proper mufflers can keep down noise, but this does not satisfy cycling's enemies.

With all this going on, it is refreshing to find that motorcycling does have its friends who are working to help keep cycling from being strangled by restrictions. One of these is California State Bureau of Land Management director J. R. Penny, who recently told a legislative committee, "The Bureau of Land Management recognizes off-road vehicle use as a valid form of public land use and does not intend to eliminate the use."

Another is Harrison Loesch, assistant secretary of the Federal Department of the Interior. The Department is responsible for management of federal public lands.

Speaking to a meeting of the Motorcycle Industry Council, Loesch said, "The motorcyclist has essentially the same rights to do his 'outdoor thing' as does the bird watcher."

He went on to say that for safety reasons "the backpacker should not have to share a trail with a cycle. And the wildlife watcher or photographer would not be expected to have his privacy invaded and the wildlife disturbed by noisy trail bikes."

The solution to the conflict between motorcyclists, hikers, and conservationists is to set aside special areas for motorcyclists. The State of California has set aside a 15,000-acre area south of Barstow in the Mojave Desert for off-road vehicles. This of course includes dune buggies, jeeps, and other recreational vehicles as well as motorcycles.

The Bureau of Land Management estimates that there are 2.5 million off-road recreational vehicles using public domain land in the eleven western states. Of this total about one million are motorcycles.

There is now a plan to set aside another 100,000 acres of federal land near San Bernardino county, California, as an additional area for off-road vehicles.

Still another happy sign which could well be followed by other cities is a minibike park opened in Anaheim, California, by the city's parks and recreation department. This 12-acre facility is open to children and adults riding bikes up to 125 cc.

It has three Moto-Cross type race tracks graded from easy to reasonably hard that can accommodate up to 150 riders. There is no age limit here as there is for street bike riders. Youngsters down to five-year-olds zip around the course on their miniature bikes. However, parents must sign waivers for minor children to protect the city against lawsuits in case of injuries. The park is open seven days a week and costs only a dollar per bike. It was built with donations from private organizations but is operated by the city.

The beauty of such an arrangement is that the park provides a place to ride for young people not old enough to qualify for drivers' licenses. The Moto-Cross-type tracks gives them experience in riding over difficult terrain, and the absolute insistence on proper safety rules provides training that will develop skilled motorcycle riders of the future.

Chapter 9

MOTORCYCLE COMPETITIONS

Thousands of motorcyclists ride all their lives without engaging in cycle competition and have a wonderful time on street, road, and off-the-road runs. However, competition is the most dramatic part of motorcycling.

Competition riding is not as dangerous as it appears. Although the spectator sees a lot of spills and is thrilled by dramatic leaps into the air and apparently reckless broadslides around turns, competition riders understand their machines and know just how far they can push them. The number of motorcycle accidents is far greater on streets and roads than on competition tracks. The reason is that a majority of accidents are caused by inattention to road hazards, poor equipment, and inexperience.

Veteran competition riders are masters at keeping attention on the business at hand. Their machines are worked and fine-tuned, and most have grown up with motorcycles so that they have the required experience. In addition, they understand the value of protective clothing.

You'll always see them with crash helmet, full leathers, and boots. Full leathers are heavy leather pants and jacket. Their heavy gloves are reinforced along the back with strips of leather or foam rubber to take up shock. Some bypass the traditional leather pants and wear padded football pants instead. One innovator, tired of being slammed by rocks thrown up by the rear wheel of other competitors, showed up at a race wearing a baseball catcher's chest protector.

Leathers are expensive. As one competitor explained it, "These pants cost me fifty bucks. The first time I wore them was on a desert cross-country run. I snagged a handlebar on a creosote bush and went right over the top. I plowed up a furrow any farmer would have been proud of and did it with my behind. The seat of my pants looked like they had been sandpapered. Right then those pants paid for themselves. I've never grumbled about the price of leathers since."

Types of Competition

Racing is the best known motorcycle competition, but it is just one of many. Several do not depend upon speed at all. One of these is Trials Riding—or Observed Field Trials, as the American Motorcycle Association officially tags it.

This is a contest over a private course laid out to include a wide variety of natural hazards one would normally meet in motorcycling. You may find on a trials course such things as a section of sand, a section of rocks, a dip with a water splash, a hill to climb, a place to test brakes, a place to test steering through narrow areas, and so on.

The object here is not to be the first through the course as in flat track racing, but to lose the least points. If run according to AMA rules, contestants start with 1,000 points. Then you start losing points. Penalties are scored

Heavy nobby tires help this trials machine dig in for traction when plowing through a sand obstacle on the course.

A representative of a cycle publication gives a demonstration of trials riding at a recent motorcycle show. Here the rider takes his Bultaco over a platform drop.

for touching the ground with the feet, stopping with one or both feet on the ground, failure to get through one of the obstacle sections, and letting either of your wheels cross the marked travel section.

If a brake test is included, then contestants roll downhill in a free coast (that is, with engine out of gear). At the bottom a "brake" line is marked about one motorcycle length in front of the "finish" line. Contestants are not permitted to hit their brakes before the brake line and must stop exactly on the finish line. There is a penalty for going over the line.

This brake test is often used as a tie-breaker for other trials events.

Trials riding is generally a slow operation, since speed can only make trouble. Trials are won by doing everything right rather than fast. As a result, trials riding is easier on machines than any other class of competition. The slow speed also rules out a lot of the danger inherent in high-speed racing. That makes trials riding a great sport for beginners to break into competition motorcycling.

Trials riders recommend lightweight machines that can turn sharply. Large sprockets on the rear wheel will gear the machine down for the slow speeds needed in trials riding.

Enduros

The Enduros—endurance runs—are another type of motorcycle competition where breakneck speed is not required. Quoting AMA, Enduros are "scheduled runs, conducted over little used roads, trails, footpaths, and all other types of terrain, just as long as it is possible to be negotiated by the power of a motorcycle, and/or the muscular energy of the contestant."

In other words, if you can't ride, get out and push the thing. Enduros differ from road runs in that the latter are restricted to automobile roads, paved, dirt, or gravel. Enduros may go anywhere a cycle can grind its way through.

The Enduro course is laid out with a motorcycle, and

checkpoints are arranged along the route. A definite running time is established between each checkpoint. The object is to arrive at each checkpoint and the finish line in the exact prescribed time. You start with 1,000 points, just as in the observed field trials. From that point on you start losing points. Scoring systems may vary, depending upon whether the club is putting on the run itself or has

The Enduro is a race over a course that goes anywhere a motorcycle should be able to go. The problem here is not speed, but consistent times between checkpoints. You win not by being first, but by losing the least number of penalty points.

been sanctioned by one of the various associations. If the latter, the race must be run according to association rules. In the former case, the club can make up any rules its members want.

As a general rule, the scoring runs like this: You are

penalized one point for each minute you are late at any checkpoint. You lose two points for each minute you are early. Then if you are fifteen minutes ahead of your schedule, you are disqualified. However, you can be as much as an hour late before you get the scorer's thumb.

This type of competition puts a premium on consistent riding, and a clock or large watch fastened between your handlebars is as necessary as your speedometer and two wheels.

Keeping On Time

It is not easy to come in exactly on the second and save penalty points. The checkpoints may vary from five to forty miles apart. At the start of the race, you are given a schedule of the checkpoints and their distances. If you were alone on the road, it would be a simple matter to take your allotted time and figure out the exact speed you must maintain to reach the checkpoint right on the second.

In practice it is not that simple. The course has been laid out over varying terrain. Remember that the rules say the course can cover any ground where a motorcycle can go. There will be places where it is impossible to maintain a set average speed. This constant changing from crawl to charge will require some fast refiguring of the speed average that you must maintain to get to the next checkpoint on time.

One way of doing this is to take your schedule and figure out how many miles or fraction of a mile you must make in a minute. Suppose you find that you must average one-half mile every minute to get in on time. This is thirty miles per hour.

As you ride along you constantly check your odometer and clock. It would be easy if you could just put the speedometer on thirty miles per hour and leave it. The constant change of speed makes this impossible. So every five minutes or so on a long run you make a check. If the clock says you've traveled for five minutes, then your odometer should show that you've covered two and a half miles. If you are late or early you can slow or speed up to get back on schedule.

Top Enduro riders often have their own private methods of keeping time which they have worked out by trial and error. Some even use two clocks. One is set for the total run time and the other used to time the laps between check points.

Catching the Sharpies

The first thing many beginners at Enduro running ask is: "Why can't I kick up my speed to insure that I will not be late and then stop a short distance from the checkpoint and wait for the clock until I can make a timed sprint into the checkpoint?"

The answer is that secret checkpoints have been set up to make things tougher. The regular checkpoint marked on riders' schedules are called "known checkpoints." The secret checkpoint cannot be closer than five miles to a known point.

These points are marked with red and white flags. The checker docks you two points for each minute you arrive early and one point for each minute you are later than your exact due time. The due time, of course, is the time the cycle that laid out the course arrived at this secret point.

Now if you come over a rise and see these flags in front of you and you know from your own clock that you are running fast, it is no good to throw on the brakes and stop. You can slow down until you are just crawling, but the second you stop forward motion, the checker's clock stops. You are timed right there.

These secret check scores are averaged in with your known check scores to get your final score.

Cross-Country Racing

In the final analysis a cross-country race is a race across country. Unfortunately for this simple explanation, riders and promotors have complicated things by making slight changes that make one race sufficiently different from another that a different name gets tagged to it.

AMA defines a Cross-Country run as "a contest over any course, preferably cross-country, where rider ability is the determining factor." That means getting across the finish line first. The rules go on to define the course as "including little-used roads, trails, footpaths, up and down hill and any other type of terrain that can be traveled."

This sounds the same as Enduro. But in Enduro you are trying to make an exact time and in Cross-Country, you are really racing your fellow riders and not the clock.

One type of Cross-Country is Hare and Hounds. These are mass-start races with as many as 1,500 machines strung out across the desert. This fantastic number of entries was actually recorded in the 1970 Barstow (California) to Las Vegas (Nevada) race. The race drew entries from all the way to the east coast. Many cyclists make the pilgrimage from the East and the Midwest where vacant land, needed for these mass desert races, is not available.

Another famous race is the Mint 400 up Nevada way. And of course the Mexican Baja classic tops them all.

The Hare and Hounds chase is not to be confused with the Hare Scrambles. They are the same except in length. The Scrambles is run where there is insufficient open space for a long race and can be as short as five miles. The course can be repeated until it totals forty actual running miles.

Scrambles

There are quite a number of events that fall into the Scrambles category beside Hare Scrambles. The European Scrambles resembles the Hare and Hounds Chase except that it is held over a closed course and with each event having a definite time limit. It is usually divided into an expert and an amateur division.

The Rough Scrambles must be at least 50 percent over improved roads and has no maximum length. The Grand Prix Scrambles is over a known, closed course, and the TT Scrambles must be 50 percent improved course and may be 100 percent improved.

TT events have been labeled by these initials so long that it is actually getting hard to find anyone who knows what they stand for anymore. It means Tourist Trophy and came from the first TT race which was run on the Isle of Man in 1907. The TT Scrambles is a short version of the TT race.

From all accounts the first TT race must have been a grand adventure, resembling today's Cross-Country. It began in the yard of a pub—an English saloon—where both machines and riders were fueled for the ordeal. And an ordeal it was.

Motorcycles then were little more than bicycles with engines. The racers left the bicycle pedals on so they could pedal if their engines failed, which happened often with those notoriously balky machines. In addition each rider stuffed saddle bags and pockets with extra plugs, tools, drive belts, chains, and tire-repair kits.

Records show that the fastest lap speed made in this pioneer race was 42.91 miles per hour. The original course was lengthened to 37½ miles in 1911 to become the "mountain course" still in use for the Isle of Man TT Races today. However, it is now paved. Then it followed an oxcart trail over the Manx moors. Reports claim the course was then as rough as today's desert runs.

Moto-Cross

One of the fastest growing competitive motorcycle sports today is Moto-Cross. Actually it is another form of Scrambles and once was called that. It is run over a closed course of roughly two miles in length, although some races are shorter. It is dirt track all the way. They are run in several heats or motos. For example, I have seen races run in three 30-minute motos. Others have run two to four 20-minute motos. Some races are run with 40-minute motos, plus a lap or two. It can be seen then that these races are run on time rather than in laps.

It is possible for a rider to come in low in one of the motos but still win the day's race if he can make up in the succeeding heats.

Moto-Cross began in the 1920's in England as "rough riding scrambles," but it was France that gave it the name

A trio of Moto-Cross riders corner a muddy turn in the 1971 opening of the INTER-AMA (International American Moto-Cross Series), at Indian Dunes, California. Note that the two cornering riders have their right legs out ready to drag their steel-shod boots to keep their bikes from lying down on the muddy, slippery turn.

of "Moto-Cross." *Moto* comes from motorcycle and *cross* means cross-country. However, because of the closed course and heat-style of racing, it is quite different from cross-country racing. The track has a succession of hazards, including mud holes.

Moto-Cross has been much more popular in Europe than in the United States, although this is changing. As a result, Europeans dominate the international Moto-Cross circuit.

In this Moto-Cross competition three cyclists fight to overtake the leader. The rough course in this fast-growing segment of motorcycling seem to keep the bikes in the air as much as they are on the ground. It is poor practice to ride with bare arms as the cyclist in the back is doing. There are many spills in this sport and competition leathers will keep a rider from leaving a lot of hide on the ground.

Drag Racing

Another up-and-coming motorcycle sport is drag racing, which is the two-wheel equivalent of the hot-rodder's favorite automobile sport. Dragging differs from other competitive sports in that it is purely an acceleration test. It is generally run over a quarter-mile course, but can be lengthened to as much as a mile.

Drags can't be run much over this because the machines have been modified for quick getaways and will burn up on long hauls.

Drag races are generally elimination contests. Two bikes run against each other. The loser is eliminated and the winner returns to run against the winner of another heat. This continues until one remains, and he is the op Eliminator or winner.

Drags are divided into various classes and the amount of permissible modification or "hopping up" is determined by the class. Both the American Hot Rod Association and the National Hot Rod Association sanction motorcycle drag; the rules depend upon which association the track is affiliated with.

Association rules vary from year to year, but presently here is the way the Motorcycle Division of the American Hot Rod Association breaks down.

A. *Dragster Bike Division.* This breaks down into four classes to accommodate exotic fuels, supercharged engines, fuel injection, etc. This class is for all-out dragsters.

B. *Modified Bike Division.* There are three classes here, determined by total cubic-centimeter dis-

This drag race machine uses two twin-cyclinder engines with a carburetor for each of the four cylinders.

Flat track motorcycle racers wear thin "leathers" for protection and ride machines with streamlined farings for less wind resistance.

Gassing up for a coming competition. The two Yamaha cycles belong to Gary and DeWayne Jones, brother-members of an internationally famous racing team.

placement of the engines. These are classes for
street machines that have been modified (hopped
up) for high-performance competition.

C. *Stock Bike Division.* There are seven classes, determined by the total cubic-centimeter displacement
of the engines. This Division is for bikes in "show-
room condition." This means only that the engine
cannot be hopped up. Some alterations are permitted, such as altered gearing, changing carburetor
jets, bobbing the front fender, and the like.

For safety AHRA demands that all bikes competing in
drag events have a self-closing throttle and kill-button
emergency ignition switch.

Each year the two associations publish their current
rules in booklets obtainable at concession shops at drag
strips affiliated with the two associations.

Racing

In the previously discussed competitions there is plenty
of room for the amateur and the strictly Sunday rider. But
when you move into all-out racing you are moving into
the two-wheeled world of the professional.

There are several types of motorcycle races. A rider
may specialize in either, but if he has dreams of becoming
the Grand National Champ of the American Motorcycle
Association he has to pile up more points than his rival.
He has to do this on the short track, the flat track, the
half-mile, mile, TT, and in the road race.

Professional dirt-track racing is generally held on half-
mile to a mile tracks. The short track is limited to quarter-
mile tracks and to machines 250 cc and below. In Europe

the road race is just what its name implies. A road is closed and becomes the track. In the United States public officials are not as cooperative. In this country road races are run on big tracks such as Daytona International Raceway where the 200-mile road race for cycles is held in March of each year.

Speed Trials

One other very specialized motorcycle competition should be mentioned—the Speed Trials. These are held each year on the famed salt flats at Bonneville, Utah. Here during Speed Week all kinds of motor-powered vehicles come with their riders who are seeking to establish world speed records in their individual classes.

The records are established by averaging two runs over a one-mile stretch. As this is written the fastest motorcycle on earth is a Harley-Davidson streamliner built by Californian Dennis Manning and powered by a Sportster engine reworked by Warner Riley of Illinois. It was driven by Cal Rayborn of San Diego, California. A special racing support team from the Harley factor was on hand to help also. The streamliner, which is enclosed in a rocketlike body, reached the amazing speed of 265.492 mph.

Chapter 10

CYCLE CARE

Up to now we have been talking about safe riding, but all the rules and tips and suggestions are for nothing if the bike itself isn't in tip-top shape.

Motorcycle maintenance and repair are not difficult to learn. If you can work on cars, your job of learning is half done. While a course in motorcycle repair is great, you can still learn enough about general automobile mechanics to give you a thorough grounding if you can't study cycle repair itself. The principle of a four-stroke engine is the same as that of an automobile engine anyway. There is some difference in the two-stroke engine, but basically the cylinders go up and down at the turn of the crankshaft just as they do in the four-stroker.

Your cycle carburetor works on the same principle as an automobile carburetor, but it's a lot simpler. The same is true of the clutch, brakes, and gears.

Now it is well to remember that we said they work on the same *principle*. This is not the same as saying that they are *identical*. They certainly are not. They are not even the same from bike make to bike make or even from model to model of the same make.

Go by the Book

The differences in engines can be learned by studying your bike's technical manual. If none is obtainable, then both the Chilton Company and Technical Publications Division of Intertec put out superior service manuals that cover a wide variety of motorcycle makes. Both these companies' manuals presuppose that the reader knows the fundamentals of mechanics. If you understand how to tighten bolts properly, how to disassemble machinery, and the basic elements of mechanics plus the names of machine parts, then these books can point you along the way. Exploded diagrams, close-up pictures of parts, and detailed instructions help make things easy.

Simple Maintenance

It is asking too much for a beginner to start making complete overhauls of his engine. But you can do minor work, tune-ups, and safety inspections.

The first thing to look for is tightness. There have been cases where bikes came all to pieces right in the middle of the road. Bolts have a way of vibrating loose. Tiny cracks can develop in any of the bike's metal parts. These can come from repeated spills or just plain metal fatigue. Such cracks can weaken parts and eventually cause them to give way at the most embarrassing times.

All these things should be checked periodically. And if you ride hard, it isn't a bad idea to make a preride check each day.

Another thing that requires constant checking is your tires. Here your problem is a bit different from a motorists' problem. Cornering causes hard wear on the sides of a motorcycles' front tire. This is because the tire pushes against the road to keep you from going into a slide on the curves. In time the sides become more worn than the center because the sides take more strain in turns than the center of the tire does on a straight run. When the sides are so worn, cyclists say they are "peaked." Peaked tires are dangerous, for the tread is needed on the sides to support the cycle in a turn. This is why, if you remember, the tread on cycle tires curves up on the sides more than on automobile tires.

Rear tires do not show this side wear, but wear more in the center. They should be changed before the tread is worn to the point that the tire does not grip well. Slick tires can be dangerous on slippery surfaces.

Proper preventive maintenance is the key to smooth motorcycle performance. Here a couple of riders check engine idle during a tune-up operation.

Motorcycle "garages" are often open-air affairs wherever the rider happens to be. Motorcycle repair is relatively simple and the serious rider should learn to do his own work.

Proper Tire Inflation

Proper tire inflation is of even more importance on cycles than on automobiles. Cycle tires take a beating, especially in competition, and an underinflated tire may rotate on the rim under the pull of heavy traction. This can tear off a valve stem, resulting in an instant flat and a ruined tube.

Underinflation also causes excessive tread wear, makes steering difficult, and generates heat (through excessive flexing of the casing) that can cause an early tire failure.

Overinflation is also bad. A tire with too much air does not hold the road well, bounces too much, and gives a hard ride. Since there is less given in an overinflated tire, road shocks tend to damage the tire more than a properly inflated tire.

A rider should follow the tire manufacturer's recommendations on how many pounds of air to carry in his tires. This will vary according to the loads the cycle carries. If you carry a passenger on the pillion seat or a heavy load, then it will be necessary to increase inflation to keep the tires from flattening out under the load. Otherwise the results will be the same as underinflation with a normal load.

The manufacturer's recommendations should be followed as to the amount of pressure to increase for loads. This may vary with different manufacturers. As a general guide, the recommended pressure for the Truimph 650-cc is 24 pounds pressure for the front and 25 pounds for the rear tire with a normal load. If a passenger is carried, the company recommends a four-pound step-up for the front tire and an additional six pounds in the rear where most of the extra weight is carried.

Harley-Davidson recommends 14 pounds for the front and 18 pounds for the rear on their Sportster model. To this you add one pound for each 50 pounds of rider weight above 150 pounds for the front tire and two pounds for each 50 pounds of riders weight for the rear tire.

Troubleshooting

Motorcycle manufacturers and salesmen are great hands for telling us how easily their machines start. Unfortunately, there comes the time when we pound the kick starter until we are red in the face and nothing happens.

This is not so bad—although expensive—if there is a motorcycle garage around the corner. It is not so good if you are trail riding, desert scrambling, or touring miles and miles from town. Therefore, every rider should know something about engine troubleshooting, for many of the things that keep an engine from starting can be easily corrected if one just knows how.

When an engine fails to start, it can generally be traced to just two things: either the engine is not getting gas or it is not getting spark. Simple enough? Well, it would be except there are quite a number of things that cause these two fundamental troubles.

Fuel Troubles

Let's start with the gas problem. Gasoline comes from the tank into the carburetor where it is mixed with air and fed into the cylinder to be ignited by the spark plug.

When a cycle fails to start, the first place to check is the gas tank. Is it empty? Quite a number of times this is the cause of the trouble. Next remove a spark plug and turn over the engine. You can generally smell gasoline if the mix is getting into the cylinder. Sometimes, if the engine is flooded, the plug ends may be wet with gas. The plugs will not fire in this condition.

If no gas is getting to the cylinder, the trouble may be one of these causes:

- You let the gas tank go dry.
- You forgot to turn on the fuel shut-off valve.
- The fuel tank vent may be clogged. You must get air into the tank for the gas to flow out.
- The carburetor may be out of order, lines plugged, float stuck, lines not tight, jets clogged, etc.
- The choke may not be operating properly.

If you are getting the proper gas mixture to the cylinders, then check out the spark. The gas mixture cannot ignite unless there is a sufficiently strong spark leaping the gap between the plug electrodes.

This can be checked by a trick so old it was in use by stranded motorists back when the Model T was a pup. Remove the spark plug wire and hold it close to the bare metal of the engine. If the spark is good, you should see a spark jump the gap between the wire and the metal when the engine is turned over.

- If you get no spark, then your trouble may be among these items:
- If battery ignition type, you may have a run-down battery.

- If magneto type, then you may have an incorrect gap between your primary coil and the flywheel magnets. Or you may have one of the following:
- Improperly adjusted or burned ignition points.
- Loose wires or malfunctioning ignition switch.
- Condenser out.
- Bad coil.
- Spark plugs fouled or improperly gapped.

Most of these items can be corrected in the field. If points are burned, you can sometimes scrape them with a penknife and get enough fire through to get you home. Plugs can be cleaned and regapped. Loose wires can be tightened and broken wires patched up. If the condenser is the trouble, you can sometimes get home on it just by cleaning the points. The purpose of the condenser is to absorb extra electricity to keep the points from arcing and burning. If a coil goes out (not a common occurrence), then you are stuck with a replacement.

Frayed Cables

Engine troubles are not the only disasters that can befall a cycle a long way from home. The front-brake cable and the clutch cable are sometimes the source of trouble.

These cables generally consist of woven wire inside a protective tubing. They are naturally subject to wear, especially where they join the brake and clutch lever. However, a partially broken or frayed cable inside the tubing can sometimes cause the cable to stick. The same thing is true of the throttle cable. It can readily be seen that if you can't shift, brake, or change your engine speed when you need to, then you no longer have control of your machine and you are in trouble.

This means that cables should be periodically inspected and changed at the first sign of wear. It is false economy to try and make a cable last a little longer. This is something the rider, however inexperienced he may be in mechanics, can easily do himself.

Check Your Chains

Most motorcycles are run by chains. There is a chain from the primary sprocket (the one run by the engine) and another chain from the primary sprocket to the final drive sprocket on the rear wheel.

One of the most important preventive maintenance checks that a motorcycle owner can make is to keep an eye on the condition of his cycle's chains.

Although they look comparatively simple, sprockets and chains are very carefully designed. Chain pitch must equal sprocket pitch. The chain pitch is the distance from the exact center of the depression between two sprocket teeth to the exact center of the depression between the next two teeth. The pitch of the chain is the distance between the center of the bearing at one end of the link to the center of the bearing at the opposite link.

If the pitch of the two are equal, the chain will move around the sprocket evenly and with a minimum of friction. The chain load is evenly distributed over several sprocket teeth.

This chain-sprocket pitch relationship changes as sprocket and chain wear. When this happens, instead of the chain roller falling directly into the center of the depression between the sprocket teeth, it hits part way up on the tooth. This causes excessive wear that can quickly ruin a chain.

Ordinarily chains are replaced when the "stretch" is more than one-quarter inch per foot. Sprockets are replaced when a visual inspection shows they are worn. If the wear is on the outside of the sprocket, then the trouble is due to bad alignment between sprocket and chain.

All mechanics agree that you should never replace a chain without replacing the sprocket also, for if one is worn more than the other you soon ruin the replacement.

Chain Free Play

If the chain is too tight, it will also cause a quick wearout. There should be a certain amount of free play in the chain. The amount of free play is indicated by how much you can lift up the chain from its normal riding position, and is specified by the manufacturer. The Harley-Davidson 74 OHV calls for one-half-inch free play. The Triumph 230 and 500 Twins want three-quarter-inch, and the Honda asks for between one-half- and three-quarter-inch.

Free play can be adjusted by loosening an adjusting nut on the rear wheel and tightening or loosening an adjuster nut (see illustration).

While the entire bike must be lubricated periodically in accordance with the manufacturer's specifications, the chain is a special source of lubrication problems.

Lubrication of the engine itself is no problem. You either add oil to the oil tank if the machine has one, and mix oil with the gasoline if it does not have a separate oil tank. Wheel bearings, cables, and other moving parts also must be lubricated. Most of these items are enclosed where the oil or grease is protected. But the chain—on most models—is out in the open.

This means that the lubrication is not only subject to deterioration from the elements but also picks up dirt and grit which will wear out chain and sprocket in a hurry.

There is nothing to do about this except keep the bike clean and relubricate when necessary. Chains take a special grease lubrication and it must work itself down inside the chain to lubricate the interior moving parts of the links.

Cleanliness cannot be overemphasized. And it has nothing to do with dressing well to keep the neighbors from otherwise assuming you are a filthy bum. You must keep the *bike* clean to avoid wearing it out before its time. Cleanliness is also a safety factor. If your gearshift lever, brake pedal, or handlebars are greasy, there is always the danger of a foot or hand slipping at a crucial moment either on the road or in a race.

Chain pitch is the distance between the center of the chain bushings as shown in circle A. Sprocket-tooth pitch is the distance between the center of a sprocket tooth to the center of the adjoining sprocket tooth as shown in circle B. Number 1 in circle C is the adjusting nut and number 2 is the adjuster to regulate free play of the rear chain.

If dirt and grease get in between the fins of your engine, you may find yourself with an overheating problem. The only way your engine has to get rid of the heat generated by its internal combusion is to radiate it to the air blowing through the fins. If dirt and grease build up in the spaces between the fins, you don't get the full cooling effect of the air. Then your engine overheats and may even get to the point where the metal, expanding under the extra heat, will seize (bind) and stop completely.

Other Things to Watch

Even if one is not qualified to do one's own major maintenance, it is well to keep an eye on the bike's total performance and take it to a qualified mechanic when performance begins to drop. It is important that each engine get proper tune-ups which check the points in the distributor, clean and adjust the spark plugs, check the strength of the coil, clean and readjust the carburetor, and check the engine for carbonization.

As noted in Chapter 1, gasoline is chemically a hydro-carbon. It so happens that in combustion the hydrogen part of the chemical combination burns more easily and carbon deposits are left in the engine.

This deposit of carbon can have two major effects on an engine. Tiny bits of carbon in the combustion chamber can keep glowing red hot and cause the new gas mixture to ignite from the carbon before spark plugs can cause ignition at the proper timing interval. As we have seen, this is called *preignition.* Thus the burning gas starts to expand and pushes down on the piston while the crank-shaft is still forcing the piston up from the last stroke. The least this can do is cause loss of power. The worst is to tear up the engine. This same effect can also be caused, as explained earlier, by improper engine timing.

The second major trouble that carbonization of an engine can cause is to choke up the exhaust port so that the exhaust gases have difficulty getting out of the engine.

Sometimes a fast run can help blow some excess carbon out through the exhaust pipe, but for a complete solution the engine must be dismantled and the carbon removed by hand. It is important in carbon removal not to score or scratch ports, cylinder walls, and pistons in the cleaning process.

Chapter 11

A FINAL WORD

When you make the plunge and buy your first motorcycle what do you think of? The first thing is who will ride it. For a child the rule is nothing bigger than one which will permit his feet to touch the ground. If the rider is a woman or a girl, a light machine is better because she can get it up if she skids. I know one woman rider who told me flatly she could ride any machine a man can. I don't doubt her word, but for most feminine riders it is best to stick to a light machine.

For a man the first thing to consider is your desires. What do you want the bike for? You don't want a big 1200 cc cruiser for trail bike riding. And you don't want a 125 cc job for road touring. Buy what fits your purpose. It is poor economy to buy less than what you want with the intention of trading up later. You generally lose money every time you trade.

What Will It Cost?

As for prices, you can get mini-bikes in the hundred-dollar-plus range. You can drive a 125cc machine for something less than $500, a 250cc for around $750 and up, and the big cruisers run from $1500 to $2000. Custom bikes can cost a fortune.

These were general prices when this was written. They will constantly change. You can also figure on from $60 to $200 extra for insurance. If you are under twenty-one, insurance may be prohibitively high in some areas. At this age your parents will also have to sign your applications. With changes now coming into effect this requirement may be cut to 18 years in many localities.

One way to get around high prices of cycles is to buy a second-hand machine. You can get good deals if you stick with reputable dealers.

What to Look For

The first thing to do is make a careful inspection of the frame, fork, and suspension, looking for cracks, dents, and sags. Check the brake and clutch pedals. If you have to push all the way down on the rear-brake pedal to make it hold, or if when you squeeze the front-brake or clutch lever the lever lies back against the handlebar grip, then you know this is the same as in a car when the brake squishes all the way to the floorboard. Something is definitely wrong.

Next try all the controls. Do they work smoothly? This includes the hand and foot controls—brakes, clutch, gearshift, and even the ignition switch and headlight switch.

Start up the engine. Does it start quickly? A tendency to start hard or idle rough may mean carburetor jets are worn. Does it take gas smoothly? How does it start moving? Like a jackrabbit? Or do you glide off from your stop? How is the pickup?

Listen to the engine. Better still, listen to several engines. Do you hear any strange noises in yours that are not present in the others? Do you hear a preignition ping? This could mean that the engine needs either a tune-up or a decarbon job.

After you take the cycle on a test run to check its acceleration and balance, remove a spark plug when you get back. Even though the plug may have been cleaned when the machine was put on the lot, if the engine is in really bad shape even your short run may show deposits on the ends of the plugs. An experienced mechanic can tell a lot about an engine from inspecting the plugs.

If the plug has a damp sludgy deposit, it could mean that the poor oil control is caused by worn valve guides, worn or broken piston rings, or even a worn cylinder bore (hole).

A fluffy black appearance to the plug terminals could be caused by the wrong kind of plug (too cold), carburetor choke out of adjustment, or carburetor too rich (too much gas for the amount of air). A dirty air filter will also cause the gas mixture to be too rich by obstructing some of the air to the carburetor.

Spotty carbon deposits on the plug indicate that new plugs have recently been installed in an engine that needs a carbon removal job.

The fact that you find something wrong does not necessarily mean that the bike is a bad buy. The deciding point is the price and your willingness to make repairs. Some of the things you find wrong may be easily repaired by yourself with little trouble. In such cases, if the price is right, you are well advised to buy. On the other hand, it is well to avoid buys that will run into major overhauls.

A lot depends upon your purpose. I know one man and his son who buy nothing but wrecks. They are customizers, and no matter what kind of a machine they start with they end up with something the manufacturer would never recognize as the original product. Customizing is a field all its own and the results are beautiful to behold. The prices on these finished beauties are in the Cadillac-and-up class. Custom bikes are often only for shows and are not intended to be ridden. After all, who is going to risk scratching the chrome on an $8,000-up beauty?

On Your Way

Somewhere between the range of a hundred dollars for a secondhand minibike to $8,000 for a customized dreamboat, just about everyone can find something in the price range that will permit him to join the wonderful world of two-wheel fun. And fun it is. There is something about zipping along with the wind whipping about you, and with your body so tuned to the machine that the two of you seem like one, that produces a thrill no other type of riding can.

While competition cycling gets the publicity and the one-percenters (as cyclists call the long-hair black-jacket rough riders) get movies made about them, the majority of the nation's millions of cyclists are riding just for the fun it. When you join them you are getting in with a gang numbering two million plus. And this multimillion figure is just for registered bikes. Including off-road and minibikes that don't require registering, there are probably nearly two and a half million fun riders to a half-million competitors.

So the accent is on fun. But to have fun on a cycle you must follow the safety rules. In cycling, safety and fun are joined together just as firmly as the links in the chain that drives your cycle.

I remember the man who sold me my first bike, an Indian motorcycle, thirty years ago. He said as I got in the saddle to drive off, "Have fun—and *drive safely.*"

He summed it up well in those five words.

Glossary

back shafting   shifting the transmission to a lower gear; also called *down-shifting.*

BDC   bottom dead center or the lowest point a piston can descend in a stroke of an internal combustion engine.

bike   popular nickname for motorcycle.

broadsliding   a sidewise slide; may be accidental or done on purpose by racing drivers as an aid in fast cornering.

cam   camshaft.

camshaft   a metal shaft with lobes which operate valve lifters in four-stroke engines.

carb   carburetor.

celerifère   walking machine invented in 1690; forerunner of both the bicycle and the motorcycle.

cubes   cubic centimeter displacement of a motorcycle engine. An engine's total of cubes is the sum of the cubic volume of all its cyclinders.

customize   To restyle in an individualistic manner.

Draisienne   Improved walking machine invented in 1816.

drag racing   An acceleration contest between two vehicles, usually run over a quarter-mile course. Both the National Hot Rod Association and the American Hot Rod Association have classes for drag-racing motorcycles.

E.T. elapsed time; the time it takes drag-racing vehicles to get from the start to the finish lines.

Enduro cross-country motorcycle runs where the winner is determined by whoever loses the least number of points from a starting 1,000 points.

English trials a test of driver skill in crossing rough terrain. Riders are penalized for touching the ground with their feet, crossing marked lines, etc.

fairing streamlined shield used on front of motorcycles.

field meet series of games and sports.

fins cooling areas of a motorcycle. Heat generated by the internal combustion engine is radiated by the fins as air blows through them.

flat track An oval, closed race track; generally a dirt track.

four-stroke A type of internal combustion engine which requires four strokes of the piston for each firing of the gas-air mixture.

Hare and Hounds Race over open ground.

head cylinder head.

hog or road hog heavyweight motorcycle, especially an older model.

hot shoe a reckless rider.

knobs or knobby tires with large cleats of rubber, useful in traveling over sand or soft ground.

leathers leather clothing worn in competition motorcycling.

loop action of a motorcycle looping or rearing back on its driver. It can be caused by a too fast start or when climbing an incline that is too steep for the vehicle.

lunger, also one-lunger one-cylinder motorcycle engine.

magneto magnet-and-coil device attached to flywheels to generate electricity or current for engines that are not equipped with batteries.

Moto-Cross a short race, generally, up to two miles in length, over a series of hazards on a dirt track.

pillion seat a separate seat in the rear of a cycle for a passenger.
pot carburetor.

road race race over a paved road with right and left turns. This is
in contrast to the flat track course, which is dirt with turns all in
one direction.

scramble short race over rough terrain.

T.T. Tourist Trophy race.
tail-gating Riding too close to the vehicle in front.
transfer port channel that carries the compressed air-gas mix from
the crankcase to the cylinder in a two-stroke engine.
trials see English Trials.
two-stroke engine one in which the pistons make only two
strokes for each firing of the engine.

up-shifting act of shifting to a higher gear.

wheelstand or wheelie riding on the back wheel with the front
wheel in the air.

INDEX

INDEX